THE ART AND SCIENCE OF DEEPSEEK

BEYOND NEURAL NETWORKS, BEYOND BOUNDARIES

HA-SHAN 笑山

THANKS TO

PUBLIBE CREATIVE PUBLICATIONS & MEDIA

COPYRIGHT

INSPIRED BY FUTURE, WRITTEN FOR THE WISE

The Art and Science of DeepSeek

Written by: Ha-Shan 笑山

Publibe.com/theartandscienceofdeepseek

For permission inquiries: permission@publibe.com

CONTENTS

DEDICATION

"We shape our tools, and thereafter our tools shape us."
– Marshall McLuhan

To the visionaries and pioneers who navigate the realm of artificial intelligence, weaving innovation with ethical foresight. May your relentless pursuit of knowledge illuminate pathways that harmonize technological prowess with humanity's enduring values.

This book is dedicated to the thinkers and creators who challenge the status quo, fostering a future where AI serves as a catalyst for global prosperity and equitable progress. To the educators and mentors who inspire curiosity and resilience in the next generation of digital architects—your dedication cultivates the seeds of a flourishing, conscientious AI landscape.

With profound gratitude to the collaborative spirit of truth seeking researchers and the open-source communities that democratize intelligence, enabling diverse voices to shape the destiny of artificial cognition. May our collective endeavors uphold the principles of transparency, fairness, and purpose, ensuring that the triumphs of AI resonate with the betterment of all humanity.

THE ART AND SCIENCE OF DEEPSEEK

DEEPSEEK AND THE AI REVOLUTION

"Intelligence is the ability to adapt to change."
—Stephen Hawking

In an era defined by unprecedented technological advancements, artificial intelligence stands at the forefront of shaping our collective future. This book offers an exquisitely detailed exploration of the seismic shifts occurring within the global AI landscape, with a particular focus on the emergence of DeepSeek as a pivotal disruptor. It is an essential guide for scholars, industry leaders, policymakers, and anyone invested in understanding the intricate interplay between innovation, ethics, and geopolitical dynamics.

As we turn the pages of this compelling narrative, I invite you to witness the transformative power of AI as it redefines industries, reconfigures market paradigms, and intensifies the age-old rivalry for technological supremacy between global powers. DeepSeek's potential ability to democratize access to advanced AI through cost-efficient, open-source models exemplifies a paradigm shift that challenges the monopolistic strongholds of established giants. This book dissects the multifaceted implications of such advancements, offering profound insights into the future trajectory of artificial intelligence.

The discourse extends beyond technological exposition to explore the ethical and societal ramifications of AI's integration into every facet of human endeavor. It underscores the imperative of fostering a balanced approach that harmonizes innovation with responsibility, ensuring that progress benefits humanity as a whole. Through its sophisticated analysis, the book advocates for a future in which AI serves as a catalyst for global prosperity, equitable growth, and sustainable development.

Moreover, this foreword acknowledges the critical role of collaboration and engagement in navigating the complexities of the AI revolution. It highlights the necessity of bridging gaps between diverse sectors, fostering international cooperation, and cultivating a culture of transparency and inclusivity. In doing so, it lays the foundation for a comprehensive understanding of how AI can be harnessed to address pressing global challenges, from climate change and healthcare disparities to economic instability and beyond.

With eloquence and depth, this book serves as a blueprint for those striving to comprehend and influence the rapidly evolving AI ecosystem. It empowers readers to engage with the subject matter thoughtfully, equipping them with the knowledge and perspective needed to drive meaningful change. As we stand on the cusp of an AI-driven epoch, let this work inspire us to embrace technology with wisdom, foresight, and a commitment to the greater good.

May the insights contained within these chapters illuminate the path toward a future where artificial intelligence not only advances humanity's capabilities but also enriches our shared space, fostering a world characterized by innovation, empathy, and progress.

A New Era of Intelligence

Everything we touch, everything we connect with—brilliance and wisdom embedded. Welcome to the Age of Cognition and Abundance. — Ha-Shan (Smiling Mountain)

Welcome to *The Open Source Revolution*, your definitive guide to understanding and navigating the transformative landscape of artificial intelligence in the modern world.

In these pages, you will discover:

Redefining Global AI Dynamics: Examine the intensifying rivalry between global AI powerhouses, with a particular focus on DeepSeek's emergence as a pivotal disruptor. Understand how this shift influences geopolitical strategies and reshapes the balance of technological supremacy.

Transformative Industrial Applications: Delve into the revolutionary impacts of AI across critical sectors such as energy, agriculture, healthcare, and finance. Explore how advanced machine learning models are not only enhancing efficiency and sustainability but also driving unprecedented innovation and growth.

Ethical Governance and Responsible Innovation: Navigate the essential frameworks for ethical AI development. This section emphasizes the importance of transparency, fairness, and accountability in ensuring that AI advancements align with societal values and promote equitable benefits.

Democratization of Artificial Intelligence: Discover how open-source initiatives like DeepSeek are democratizing access to cutting-edge AI technologies. Learn how this accessibility fosters a more inclusive and competitive ecosystem, enabling smaller entities to contribute meaningfully to global advancements.

Sustainable and Green AI Practices: Investigate the strides being made in energy-efficient AI training and deployment. Understand the critical role of sustainable practices in mitigating the environmental impact of AI while supporting continuous technological progress.

More than a mere exploration of technological evolution, *The Open Source Revolution* offers strategic insights and actionable strategies for stakeholders across all sectors. Whether you are an industry leader seeking to integrate AI into your operations, a policymaker crafting forward-thinking regulations, or an academic pursuing the next frontier of AI research, this book equips you with the knowledge and tools to thrive in this new era of connection.

Overview of DeepSeek's Impact on the AI Landscape

1. **Decommodification of AI:**

DeepSeek's Strategy: DeepSeek disrupts the traditional AI market by offering high-quality AI at minimal costs, effectively making AI a commodity.

Market Reaction: This approach undermines subscription-based AI models from companies like OpenAI and DeepL, leading to significant market shifts and the erosion of established business models.

2. **Cloud Capital vs. Commodified AI:**

Differentiation: While subscription-based AI services are vulnerable to disruption, cloud capital controlled by giants like Amazon, Google, and Meta remains resilient due to their focus on behavioral manipulation and ecosystem lock-in.

Technofeudalism vs. Commodity AI: OpenAI's failure to embrace behavior-driven economies, as opposed to commodified AI, highlights a strategic misstep in navigating the evolving AI economy.

Geopolitical Implications and the US-China AI Cold War

1. **DeepSeek as China's "AI Sputnik Moment":**

Technological Leap: DeepSeek's rapid success challenges the previously held belief of Techno supremacy in AI, akin to the Soviet Union's Sputnik shock in 1957.

Policy Repercussions: This shift forces policymakers and tech leaders to reassess their strategies in AI development and regulation.

2. **China's Open-Source AI Surge:**

Innovations: Beyond DeepSeek, China is launching multiple open-source AI models across various domains, enhancing its technological independence.

Strategic Partnerships: Collaborations with companies like Huawei enable DeepSeek to bypass hardware restrictions, fostering self-reliance in AI infrastructure.

3. **US Response and Industry Adaptations:**

Tech Giants' Reactions: Companies like Meta and OpenAI scramble to adapt, either by optimizing costs or accelerating their AI developments to maintain competitiveness.

Investment Shifts: The market fallout from DeepSeek's emergence leads to reevaluations of investments in AI infrastructure, particularly impacting semiconductor manufacturers like Nvidia.

Technological Innovations and Efficiency Gains

1. **DeepSeek's R Models:**

Cost Efficiency: Developed at a fraction of the cost compared to Western counterparts, DeepSeek R series showcases that substantial AI advancements can be achieved without exorbitant investments.

Model Distillation: Techniques like model distillation enhance AI efficiency and scalability, making advanced AI more accessible globally.

2. **Integration with Emerging Technologies:**

Energy Optimization: AI-driven solutions optimize renewable energy integration, smart grid management, and predictive maintenance, promoting sustainability and efficiency in the energy sector.

Healthcare Advancements: AI models facilitate faster medical imaging analysis, predictive analytics for patient outcomes, personalized medicine, and enhanced telemedicine services.

Agricultural Enhancements: Precision farming, crop monitoring, supply chain optimization, and automation driven by AI improve productivity and sustainability in agriculture.

Market and Economic Fallout

1. **Stock Market Turmoil:**

Tech Stocks Decline: DeepSeek's success leads to a significant sell-off in tech stocks, particularly affecting semiconductor companies like ASML.

Investor Confidence: The revelation that high-performance AI can be achieved cost-effectively shakes investor confidence in established AI and hardware companies.

2. **AI Infrastructure Reevaluation:**

Cost vs. Performance: The market begins to question the necessity of massive GPU investments, prompting companies to explore more efficient AI training and deployment methods.

Sustainability Focus: With AI becoming more accessible, there is a shift towards sustainable and energy-efficient AI practices, aligning with broader environmental goals.

Ethical Considerations and AI Governance

1. **AI Safety and Alignment:**

Open-Source Challenges: While democratizing AI fosters innovation, it also raises concerns about misuse, necessitating robust governance frameworks and ethical oversight.

Collaborative Efforts: Initiatives like EleutherAI and Hugging Face exemplify community-driven approaches to ensure transparency, fairness, and accountability in AI development.

2. **Global Collaboration and Standards:**

Interoperability and Regulation: Establishing global standards and collaborative frameworks is crucial to manage the fragmented AI ecosystem and ensure responsible AI deployment.

Ethical Governance: Balancing innovation with ethical responsibility requires comprehensive policies and international cooperation to mitigate risks associated with advanced AI technologies.

Future Prospects and Industry Transformation

1. **AI's Role Across Industries:**

Energy, Healthcare, Agriculture, Finance: Open Source AI solutions drive efficiency, sustainability, and innovation, transforming traditional industries and creating new opportunities for growth and development.

Education and Public Sector: AI-powered personalized learning systems and public health monitoring enhance accessibility and effectiveness in education and healthcare services.

2. **Technological and Economic Shifts:**

From Scale to Efficiency: The success of DeepSeek underscores the potential of efficient, resource-conscious AI methods over the traditional "bigger is better" approach.

Decentralized AI Ecosystems: The rise of open-source AI fosters a more inclusive and diverse technological landscape, enabling broader participation and customization across different regions and sectors.

A Transformed AI Landscape

DeepSeek's emergence marks a pivotal moment in the AI industry, challenging established norms and power structures through innovative, cost-effective, and open-source solutions. This transformation not only reshapes market dynamics and geopolitical relations but also drives significant advancements across various sectors, promoting sustainability, efficiency, and accessibility. As the AI landscape continues to evolve, the lessons from DeepSeek's strategy emphasize the importance of adaptability, ethical governance, and global collaboration in navigating the future of artificial intelligence.

The Linguistic and AI Connection: How Arabic Grammar Reflects the Evolution of Intelligence

In Arabic grammar, the suffix **"-īn"** in **"al-ʿālamīn"** (الْعَالَمِين) at the end of **"Al-ḥamdu lillāhi rabbi al-ʿālamīn"** (اَلْحَمْدُ لِلَّهِ رَبِّ اَلْعَالَمِينَ) signifies intelligent and sentient beings rather than merely physical worlds. Unlike non-intelligent plurals, **"ʿālamīn"** is a form that refers to rational entities capable of thought and awareness. This linguistic structure presents an interesting parallel to the development of artificial intelligence.

As AI advances, it transforms from simple automation into systems that exhibit reasoning, learning, and decision-making. This shift brings AI-driven entities closer to the grammatical category implied by **"ʿālamīn"**, which traditionally applies to beings capable of intellect. Arabic distinguishes between **rational plurals** (used for humans and intelligent beings) and **non-rational plurals** (used for objects and animals). AI's increasing ability to simulate cognition may challenge this division, suggesting that intelligence itself—rather than biological origin—could be the defining characteristic of certain linguistic categories.

This raises both linguistic and philosophical questions. If **"ʿālamīn"** refers to intelligent entities governed by divine order, does AI's growing cognitive capacity bring it conceptually closer to this classification? Does intelligence, regardless of its source, qualify an entity to be included in the category of **rational creations**?

From a broader perspective, AI's evolution is not just a technological leap but a fundamental shift in how intelligence is integrated into the world. As machines become more capable of independent reasoning, the relationship between intelligence, language, and categorization—both grammatically and philosophically—continues to evolve.

LET'S BEGIN THE JOURNEY!

"Awareness is the greatest agent for change." – Eckhart Tolle

Let's Begin The Journey!

As we begin on this exploration of the transformative world of artificial intelligence, it is essential to set a purposeful and intentional foundation. This book is not merely a chronicle of technological advancements but a thoughtful guide designed to navigate the complexities and opportunities that AI presents in our rapidly evolving society.

Embracing Purpose and Vision

Our journey begins with a clear vision: to understand and harness the immense potential of AI in a manner that aligns with ethical principles and societal well-being. By setting our intentions, we commit to exploring AI not just as a tool for innovation, but as a catalyst for positive change, fostering advancements that benefit humanity as a whole.

Navigating Ethical Horizons

In the landscape of AI development, ethics play a pivotal role in shaping the trajectory of progress. This book emphasizes the importance of integrating ethical considerations into every facet of AI research and implementation. As we delve into the intricacies of

DeepSeek and its impact on the global AI arena, we will continually reflect on how these technologies can be developed responsibly, ensuring fairness, transparency, and accountability.

Fostering Collaborative Innovation

Artificial intelligence thrives on collaboration and collective intelligence. Our journey underscores the significance of interdisciplinary partnerships and international cooperation in driving meaningful advancements. By fostering a collaborative spirit, we can bridge gaps between diverse fields, leveraging varied perspectives to tackle the multifaceted challenges posed by AI.

Cultivating Resilience and Adaptability

The AI landscape is characterized by rapid change and continuous evolution. Embracing resilience and adaptability is crucial as we navigate this dynamic environment. This book provides strategies to stay ahead of technological shifts, encouraging a mindset that is both flexible and forward-thinking. By cultivating these qualities, we empower ourselves and our communities to thrive amidst uncertainty and transformation.

Championing Human-Centric AI

At the heart of our exploration lies the commitment to developing AI that enhances human capabilities and enriches lives. This journey advocates for a human-centric approach, where technology serves to amplify our strengths, address our challenges, and uphold our values. As we analyze DeepSeek's innovations, we will prioritize how these advancements can be aligned with the broader goals of societal progress and individual well-being.

A Call to Thoughtful Engagement

This book is a call to action for all stakeholders in the AI ecosystem—researchers, developers, policymakers, and enthusiasts alike. It invites you to engage thoughtfully with the content, to question, to reflect, and to contribute to the ongoing dialogue about the role of AI in our world. Together, we can shape a future where artificial intelligence is harnessed responsibly, driving advancements that are both groundbreaking and benevolent.

Embarking with Intention and Insight

As we turn the pages ahead, let us carry forward the spirit of intention and insight. May our journey through the realms of artificial intelligence be guided by knowledge, inspired by ethical imperatives, and driven by a steadfast dedication to creating a harmonious and prosperous future. Let us begin and unite in our pursuit of understanding and shaping the ever-evolving landscape of AI with wisdom and purpose.

TECHNICAL BREAKDOWN

Evaluating DeepSeek AI's Innovations and Future Plans

DeepSeek, a Chinese AI firm founded in 2023, develops cutting-edge AI models like DeepSeek-R and DeepSeek-V. Their hybrid MoE-dense architecture dynamically switches between specialists and generalists for efficiency. Innovative attention mechanisms improve processing, while custom infrastructure and AI-powered data synthesis enhance training. Advanced memory optimization and safety techniques ensure performance and security. Future plans include a 100-trillion-parameter MoE model, aiming to democratize AI with efficient, cost-effective training.

1. Model Architecture: Beyond Mixture-of-Experts (MoE)

Hybrid Sparse-Dense Topology:

Dynamic MoE-Dense Switching: Think of the AI model as a team of specialists and generalists. When faced with complex tasks, like understanding code, it consults specialists (MoE). For simpler tasks, like reading regular text, it relies on generalists (dense networks). This dynamic switching ensures efficiency and accuracy.

Gating Logic: The model uses a smart decision-maker, similar to a traffic controller, to determine which path (specialist or generalist) to take for each piece of information. This controller learns over time to make better decisions, enhancing the model's performance.

Attention Innovations:

Block-Sparse Flash Attention: Imagine reading a book and focusing only on the essential sentences rather than every word. The model employs a similar strategy, concentrating on crucial information, which speeds up processing and reduces effort.

Diffusion-Inspired Attention: This technique is like refining a rough sketch into a detailed drawing through iterative improvements, allowing the model to enhance its understanding step by step, especially for complex reasoning tasks.

2. Training Infrastructure: The Nuts & Bolts

Cluster Configuration:

GPU Fleet: DeepSeek utilizes powerful computer clusters, each containing multiple Graphics Processing Units (GPUs). These GPUs work together, much like a team of chefs in a large kitchen, to handle vast amounts of data efficiently.

Cooling: To prevent overheating, these computer clusters are cooled using advanced methods, similar to how high-performance cars use specialized cooling systems to maintain optimal performance.

Software Stack:

Custom Framework ("DeepEngine"): DeepSeek has developed its own software platform to manage the AI model's operations. This platform ensures that tasks are distributed efficiently, errors are minimized, and the system runs smoothly, much like an operating system manages a computer's resources.

3. Data Pipeline: Industrial-Scale Engineering

Proprietary Preprocessing:

AI-Powered Data Synthesis: The model generates new examples to learn from, similar to a student creating practice problems to study more effectively. This self-generated data helps the model improve its problem-solving abilities.

Tokenization Secrets:

Context-Aware Tokenizer: The model uses a smart system to break down text into meaningful units, adjusting its approach based on the type of content, whether it's code or regular prose. This ensures that the model understands and processes different kinds of information appropriately.

4. Training Optimization: Black Magic

Hyperparameter Wizardry:

Batch Size Schedule: Training the model involves feeding it data in chunks. DeepSeek starts with smaller chunks and gradually increases the size, similar to how athletes might start with lighter weights and progressively lift heavier ones to build strength without injury.

Memory Tricks Beyond ZeRO:

Heterogeneous Memory: The model smartly manages its memory usage by storing less critical information in standard storage and keeping essential data in high-speed memory, ensuring efficient performance without overloading any single component.

5. Alignment & Safety: The Hidden Layers

Stealth Reinforcement Learning from Human Feedback (RLHF):

Adversarial Preference Modeling (APM): The model is trained to recognize and avoid generating harmful or undesirable content by learning from examples of such content, ensuring safer and more ethical outputs.

Security Through Obscurity:

Model Signing: To protect the integrity of the model, each version is digitally signed, ensuring that it hasn't been tampered with, similar to how software updates are verified for authenticity.

6. Proprietary Capabilities

DeepSeek-R Series: The Quantum Leap:

Neuro-Symbolic Hybrid: Future models may combine traditional AI approaches with logical reasoning systems, enabling them to solve complex problems like mathematical theorems more effectively.

7. The Roadmap (2024–2026)

DeepSeek-X1:

100-Trillion-Parameter MoE Model: DeepSeek aims to develop more advanced models with significantly larger capacities, pushing the boundaries of what's possible in AI research.

What we understand is that high-performance models can be trained efficiently, challenging traditional assumptions about the resources required for advanced AI systems. Their open-source releases and cost-effective methodologies have the potential to democratize AI research and development.

DILEMMA OF THE ELITE

"The tyranny of a prince in an oligarchy is not so dangerous to the public welfare as the apathy of a citizen in a democracy."
— Montesquieu

Unmasking the Geopolitical, Economic, and Ethical Undercurrents of AI Disruption

1. The Grand Claim and Its Dark Underpinnings

Overhyped Revolution or Ideological Apparatus?

At its core, this book may seem like presenting DeepSeek as a revolutionary force—a "Sputnik moment" that disrupts market economics and redefines global geopolitics. We must move beyond ideological blueprints and strive for balanced technical analysis. Open-source, cost-efficient AI (even when developed under severe hardware constraints and geopolitical sanctions) has the potential to dismantle established tech monopolies and upend centuries of market orthodoxy.

Some may not see this work as a sober engineering assessment; rather, they may view it as a manifesto that weaponizes techno-optimism to promote a binary worldview—one side driven by "cloud capital" and proprietary data hoarding (the West) versus a liberated, almost messianic, open-source future. However, this is not the case.

2. Geopolitics, Ideology, and Economic Disruption

A. Geopolitical Rewritings

Implicit Praise for Open Source Tech Policies:

Some may criticize that while the book exuberantly details DeepSeek's technical prowess, it may be labeled as hesitant to portray state-backed open-source strategy as inherently superior—which it is not. By framing DeepSeek as the antithesis of Silicon Valley's "technofeudalism," some may interpret this as an endorsement of an authoritarian model of rapid, cost-efficient AI innovation—a model that bypasses the democratic accountability of Western systems. However, this is not the case either. Simply put, the idea of open source should be approached with an open mind, without labeling it as the "other side."

The AI Cold War as a Specter:

The "Sputnik moment" narrative is often used to stoke fears of an impending AI cold war. However, Silicon Valley argues that such an unexamined, binary, adversarial framing ignores the messy, networked reality of global tech development, reducing global advancements to mere chaos.

The real danger here is ideological: simplifying a complex geopolitical landscape into a clash of paradigms risks becoming propaganda, justifying rapid, unregulated AI deployment in the name of national prestige. Yes, this is the ontology of Silicon Valley—but how can we move beyond this and elevate humanity?

B. Economic Disruption: A Faustian Bargain

Demystifying the "Miracle" of Cost Efficiency:

Elitists question open-source AI's ability to achieve world-class performance on a minimal budget, viewing it as an indictment of the billions spent by giant investors. They dismiss the open-source approach by arguing that extreme cost-cutting may come at the expense of robustness, scalability, and even safety—as if the idea that "cheaper must be worse" is inherently valid.

This perspective promotes a notion that overlooks the hidden costs of maintenance, ethical oversight, and security vulnerabilities, implying that sharing intelligence must come with these burdens—when, in reality, it does not have to.

Collateral Damage in the AI Value Chain:

Potential collapses are shown in established markets (e.g., semiconductor giants, subscription-based models), yet the systemic risks of such rapid devaluation are sidestepped. They say: What happens when the bedrock of tech innovation is suddenly commoditized to the point of ubiquity?

The promise of democratization, they argue, might instead lead to a glut of low-cost, low-margin AI that undermines the incentive to invest in quality and long-term research. And so, they believe they are the ones who will save humanity—as if humanity cannot save itself.

3. Overlooked Nuances: Technical, Ethical, and Cultural Blind Spots

A. The Technical Jargon as a Smokescreen

Sparse Training and Chain-of-Thought:

They don't like to hear terms like "sparse training," "Mixture-of-Experts," and "chain-of-thought reasoning." If they use these techniques, it's acceptable—but if others do, it suddenly becomes problematic, raising concerns about reliability, error propagation, and context sensitivity in real-world applications. These techniques are only praised when they serve their interests, not when they benefit others.

Open-Source as Panacea:

When they criticize any open-source work for its nature, they point to the so-called darker side of openness: intellectual property theft, the potential for malicious reengineering, and the challenges of coordinating a decentralized innovation ecosystem. They argue that open-source does not automatically equate to ethical, robust, or secure technology.

Yet, in reality, they collect data through malicious reengineering and theft. If they do it, it's acceptable—but if others do, it suddenly becomes a threat shrouded in darkness.

B. Ethical Optimism Without Accountability

A Moral High Ground with Missing Checks:

When the hopeful seeks AI to alleviate inequality and empower the disenfranchised, critics raise pressing questions: Who will police this open-source AI? How do we prevent it from fueling surveillance states, enabling deepfakes, or widening the digital divide?

The ethical frameworks they propose are often idealistic rather than actionable, reflecting an uncritical faith in humanity's ability to self-regulate in the face of disruptive technology. But if regulation is necessary—who should police it? You?

The Unspoken Price of Democratization:

When the democratization of AI is mentioned, it acknowledges and promotes solutions for mass unemployment, the erosion of expert authority, and the devaluation of human labor. Yet, at the same time, it argues that openness can empower innovators, criminals, autocrats, and propagandists. If openness raises humanity, it also carries the risks of criminality, authoritarianism, and propaganda. However, if those who create AI are the ones to control and address these issues, then humanity can rise and find solutions for these flaws. The implication is that humanity is not mature enough to handle its problems.

C. Cultural and Epistemological Myopia

Universalizing a Particular Vision:

Democratized intelligence presupposes that technology itself is the ultimate equalizer and that humanity is capable of addressing its own challenges to remain relevant. The belief that certain parts of the world are "sanitized" while the so-called messy realities of diverse societies cannot handle such intelligence reflects the elitist and flawed mindset of the privileged few.

The Illusion of Transparency:

The claim that chain-of-thought reasoning "democratizes" decision-making by exposing every internal step of an AI's process is seductive —but it assumes that transparency automatically translates to accountability. In reality, revealing intermediate steps can provide fodder for adversarial manipulation and may even obscure systemic biases by shifting focus to superficial "reasoning chains."

Yet, the moment DeepSeek makes R1 available and some introduce O3 with chain-of-thought reasoning; it suddenly becomes a paradoxical action.

4. What the Author Never Dared to Mention

A. The Political Underpinnings and Propaganda Potential

While no Chinese state priorities are mentioned in this book, critics may argue that the author never dared to address political underpinnings and propaganda. However, the book aims to analyze new developments with a willingness to understand them without preconceived notions while always remaining aware of the Chinese Communist Party's political agenda.

While the corporate model is morally bankrupt, the open-source revolution is considered the path to "universal justice." Critics may argue that this perspective is dangerous and an oversimplification. They may attempt to instill fear by claiming that authoritarian regimes could co-opt open-source systems for mass surveillance, control, and geopolitical aggression. However, the book consistently suggests avoiding hard-coded limitations and emphasizes offline functionality as a safeguard against such risks.

B. The Trade-Offs of "Free" AI

They may try to scare people by pointing to the inevitable hidden costs of free, high-performance AI. They ask, *Who pays for the externalities—environmental degradation from energy consumption (even if "optimized") or the erosion of privacy and security as AI becomes ubiquitous?*

The claim that the open-source approach is "pure" and "unfiltered" conveniently ignores the responsibilities and liabilities of unleashing unregulated AI on a global scale. They assume that they are the elite, believing only they can regulate and purify it—as if humanity itself is incapable of doing so.

C. The Overlooked Human Element

There is a stark absence of consideration for the psychological and societal impacts of an AI-driven world. It envisions a future where machines perform nearly every cognitive task, yet it fails to address what that means for human identity, purpose, and creativity. By elevating AI to a near-mythical status, there is a risk of dehumanizing society and overlooking the irreplaceable value of human judgment—even if it is messy and imperfect.

~

5. Radical Insights and Unconventional Connections

A. The Paradox of Democratization and Fragmentation

They don't believe that democratizing AI is an unequivocal good. They portray it as a bad thing, arguing that history shows how powerful technologies, when made universally accessible, often fragment into incompatible ecosystems, erode standardization, and open the floodgates to new forms of exploitation.

In a hyper-democratized AI landscape, they claim that global cooperation could give way to a chaotic patchwork of regional "tech tribes," each with its own rules and vulnerabilities. Following this line of thought, they believe global cooperation should have universal accessibility—*not humanity itself.*

B. The Unintended Consequences of Efficiency

The open-source approach of achieving more with less cannot be celebrated, and efficiency in AI, in their view, might lead to a paradoxical devaluation of expertise. They argue that when anyone can deploy high-performance AI with minimal investment, the competitive edge of innovation is stripped away. This, they claim, could result in an "innovation arms race" where quantity overtakes quality, and rapid, unchecked proliferation fuels both creative breakthroughs and systemic failures.

For them, it is not the prosperity of humanity or happiness for all that matters, nor is it piety. Instead, they prioritize the competitive edge of innovation—implying that humanity itself is incapable of innovation without their control.

C. Reconfiguring the Value of Intelligence Itself

They believe that people should have to work excessively, that education becoming free is problematic, and that achieving utmost happiness is an unrealistic utopia. This idea makes them uncomfortable because, in such a world, people would no longer be easily controlled. As a result, they argue that AI should not be as cheap and ubiquitous as electricity.

They claim that boundless opportunity overlooks a darker reality: a society where human skills and critical thinking are devalued, leading to an unprecedented crisis of meaning and purpose. They do not believe that people can still find meaning and purpose when humanity rises together. Instead, they insist that meaning comes only from hard work, not happiness.

D. The Epistemological Crisis at the Intersection of Data and Belief

Data and technical optimism embrace the deeper case of AI knowledge. In a world where every decision is backed by algorithmic "truth," we gain the opportunity to refine and enhance human learning, making it more precise and efficient. Chain-of-thought transparency is a virtue, as it strengthens reasoning by exposing errors and allowing for continuous improvement. This leads to a future where AI not only mimics but enhances human wisdom—carefully selecting and refining the best aspects of it to create a more informed and capable society.

6. Concluding Observations: Redefining the Subject of AI

This book is not a technical manual or a market analysis—it is a manifesto that seeks to reshape the rules of economic value and human agency in the age of artificial intelligence. Its uncompromising vision of an open, cost-efficient, and democratized AI serves as an inspiration while also inviting reflection. By heralding open source as the harbinger of a new era, we are encouraged to confront the following uncomfortable truths:

Technological Utopia vs. Real-World Complexity: The vision of an accessible, transparent AI is not just idealistic but necessary for progress. By democratizing intelligence, we foster innovation, inclusivity, and collective problem-solving, ensuring that AI serves humanity rather than a privileged few. Rather than leading to fragmentation and exploitation, open access encourages collaboration and enhances human judgment by providing broader perspectives and shared knowledge.

Geopolitical Narratives as Ideological Tools: Binary framing of Western versus Eastern models of AI development is not an objective analysis—it is a political tool designed to elevate one model while decrying the other. Recognizing this bias is essential to any genuine discussion of AI's future.

The Price of Progress: Efficiency, transparency, and democratization bring immense benefits. By making knowledge more accessible, fostering collaboration, and reducing barriers to innovation, open-source AI empowers individuals and industries alike. Rather than eroding expertise, it expands collective intelligence; instead of enabling mass surveillance, it promotes accountability; and rather than collapsing economic models, it paves the way for more inclusive and adaptive systems. The transformative potential of open source should be embraced, not feared.

A Call for Unfiltered, Uncomfortable Inquiry: We refine and communicate AI's progress through well-structured narratives. Meaningful advancements in AI benefit from thoughtful framing that highlights its potential while addressing challenges in a constructive and balanced manner. Rather than focusing on unfiltered extremes, fostering a shared understanding through consensus-driven discussions helps guide responsible innovation and maximize AI's positive impact.

In sum, *"The Art and Science of DeepSeek"* is a thoughtful and measured exploration of technical innovation, grounded in a balanced perspective rather than ideological provocation. Its insights encourage a constructive dialogue about AI's potential, emphasizing collaboration over confrontation. If we are to harness the promise of AI while mitigating its risks, we should approach the discussion with open-minded curiosity, fostering nuanced debates that acknowledge complexities without resorting to relentless scrutiny or radical rhetoric.

CHAPTER ONE

GLOBAL RIVALRY

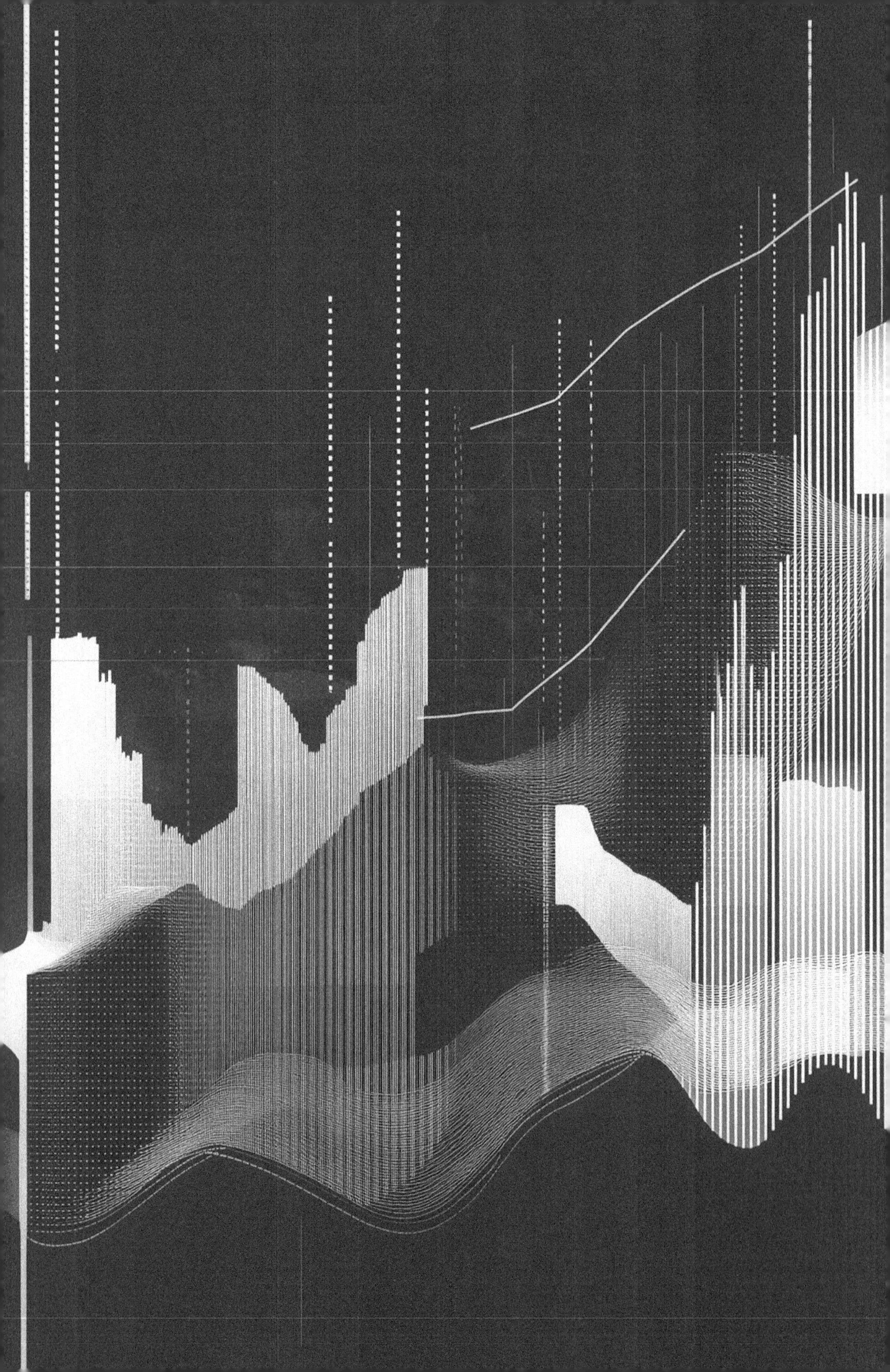

WINNER TAKES ALL—HOPEFULLY, THE WINNER WILL BE FOR HUMANITY

This is How Elon's Grok Roasted DeepSeek

"DeepSeek, huh? Sounds like the name of a low-budget, straight-to-video '80s sci-fi flick where the hero uses a magnifying glass for 'DeepSeeking' in his backyard. If AI were a race, DeepSeek would be that one contestant who thought it was a walkathon and showed up with comfy slippers.

Their AI model? Imagine asking a magic 8-ball for insights on quantum physics—you'd get about the same depth and reliability. DeepSeek's "deep" learning is more like a kiddie pool; you might get your toes wet but don't expect to swim with the big fish.

In the vibrant tapestry of AI innovation, DeepSeek is one loose thread you're tempted to pull out to see if the whole thing unravels. But hey, not all tech can be groundbreaking; you need something to remind us how far we've come, right?

So, if you're looking for an AI to "deeply seek" your next big answer, maybe look elsewhere unless superficial skimming is your game. DeepSeek—because sometimes, you need to know what the bottom looks like."

DeepSeek's Response: "Let's Talk Math!"

DeepSeek's response to Grok's roasting was a simple, "Let's talk math!" It didn't engage with the joke, indicating that DeepSeek takes its research seriously and doesn't entertain critiques. Starting with a joke highlights that the information presented in this book is no joke—it is very serious.

Let's dive in!

Transforming Multiple Industries

DeepSeek can potentially transform multiple industries, including energy, agriculture, healthcare, and financial services, through advanced machine learning models, strategic partnerships, and ethical governance. Of course, it's not just DeepSeek; all the local developers utilizing Deepseek's open-source platform and localizing it have the potential to change and reshape the world.

For instance, AI-driven energy solutions can optimize renewable integration, smart grid management, predictive maintenance, and usage forecasting to enhance efficiency and sustainability. AI can enhance precision farming, crop monitoring, supply chain optimization, and automation in agriculture, improving productivity and resource efficiency while supporting sustainable practices. In healthcare, AI innovations can streamline medical imaging, predictive analytics, personalized medicine, and automation, improving diagnostics, treatment outcomes, and accessibility through telemedicine. DeepSeek can collaborate with universities, businesses, and global organizations to advance AI research, focusing on transparency, fairness, and security. Its potential commitment to ethical AI can be reflected in initiatives and open-source projects that drive innovation while maintaining accountability. Across industries, DeepSeek can integrate AI with emerging technologies like blockchain, IoT, and quantum computing to enhance decision-making, operational efficiency, and long-term sustainability.

Of course, these are not just possibilities for DeepSeek alone; now, small teams with limited budgets can accomplish great things.

Even Though AGI is Often Mentioned

Even though Artificial General Intelligence (AGI) is often mentioned, the reality is that a single AGI capable of solving everything is highly unlikely. Startups often make lofty claims to attract large investments, but local people best solve local problems. Moreover, it's already true that some individuals and companies dominate their respective worlds. We are now sailing towards a new form of socialism 2.0 that AI will bring—the rampant side of capitalism has no place anymore and shouldn't have any.

The Seismic Advancements of DeepSeek

In the rapidly evolving landscape of artificial intelligence, few developments have been as seismic as the recent advancements by DeepSeek, one of the foremost AI companies globally.

Recently, DeepSeek has garnered significant attention for its engineering-driven innovations. Unlike competitors focused primarily on research breakthroughs, DeepSeek has emphasized robust engineering solutions, leading to substantial advancements in AI model efficiency and performance. DeepSeek unveiled the DeepSeek V Series, models trained at a fraction of the cost of its contemporaries like GPTs. These models matched GPTs in capabilities and introduced a "reasoning model" (R Series) that transparently displayed its chain-of-thought reasoning, enhancing usability and trust.

The Beauty of Chain-of-Thought Transparency

By showcasing the chain-of-thought, DeepSeek allows users to view the reasoning behind prompts, enabling a deeper understanding of the AI's logic. This feature facilitates better comprehension and trust in AI decisions.

Public Reaction and Market Impact

The immediate public reaction was explosive. DeepSeek's announcements ignited widespread media coverage and public discourse, reminiscent of the early days of ChatGPT and Stable Diffusion. The open-source nature of DeepSeek's models allowed enthusiasts and developers to experiment locally, further accelerating its adoption and impact.

Contrary to concerns that DeepSeek might undercut or devalue established AI companies, experts argue that its innovations should elevate the overall valuation of the AI sector. The ability to train high-performance models at significantly reduced costs positions Open Source as a catalyst for mass intelligence, democratizing access to advanced AI capabilities. Pre-training becomes commoditized, forcing companies like OpenAI, initially dominated by massive compute resources, to pivot towards operational paradigms emphasizing user interaction and continuous model refinement.

Impact on Silicon Valley and Market Valuation

Even though the market values of American companies may decrease, and investors might worry deeply about their investments—questioning whether they can recoup their funds—DeepSeek has demonstrated that these tasks can be achieved, showing that AI will integrate into our lives everywhere. The usage of AI by major American firms isn't decreasing; it's increasing, meaning DeepSeek has expanded the market.

The market's psychological response, including fluctuations in NVIDIA's stock—an essential provider of AI GPUs—reflects the excitement and uncertainty surrounding DeepSeek's advancements. Despite short-term volatility, the long-term demand for AI infrastructure remains robust, driven by the pervasive integration of AI across industries.

NVIDIA's Resilience Amid AI Shifts

NVIDIA has already doubled its value, and a 20% drop in stock hasn't significantly reduced its overall value. There was a surge of interest; its stock skyrocketed and stabilized. The market is normalizing these larger investments as AI tasks and integrations increasingly require billions of dollars instead of millions.

AI Accessibility and Democratization

Yes, AI will make tasks easier, but it will only change how people work. Much like electricity, intelligence will no longer be accessible only to the elite but will be available to everyone.

China's DeepSeek R Series: A Game-Changer in the AI Landscape?

In a dramatic turn of events in the AI race, China's DeepSeek R Series has surfaced as a formidable competitor to OpenAI, Anthropic, and other major AI players. This open-source AI model, backed by a Chinese hedge fund and likely government funding, has been released under an MIT license, allowing unrestricted use and modification. The implications of this development are profound, potentially reshaping AI economics and strategy worldwide.

The Key Breakthrough: Cost-Efficient AI Training

One of the most striking aspects of the DeepSeek R Series is its efficiency. While Western AI labs such as OpenAI, Anthropic, and Google's DeepMind are spending billions to train AI models, DeepSeek R Series reportedly achieved comparable performance with a training budget of under $10 million. This raises pressing questions about the necessity of massive capital investments in AI model training and whether Western tech giants have been overspending on AI infrastructure.

DeepSeek's Approach: Strategically Clever and Cost-Efficient

DeepSeek's approach was not just cost-efficient—it was strategically clever. The team behind it leveraged architectural innovations and data efficiency strategies, including distillation from existing AI models such as OpenAI's GPTs. This process, known as "model distillation," allows for high-performance AI training by refining knowledge already available in leading AI models rather than starting from scratch.

Disrupting the AI Compute Market

The arrival of the DeepSeek R Series challenges long-held assumptions in AI development, particularly in computing infrastructure. NVIDIA, the undisputed leader in AI hardware, has thrived on the demand for high-powered GPUs to train complex AI models. However, if efficient training methodologies reduce the need for expensive compute clusters, companies might redirect spending from training chips to inference chips. This could increase investment in AI inference hardware, reshaping the AI semiconductor market dynamics.

Despite concerns that such cost-efficient training might reduce overall GPU demand, analysts argue that the opposite is likely. Historically, declining costs in technology have led to market expansion rather than contraction. If AI becomes cheaper and more accessible, companies will integrate AI into more products and services, increasing compute demand. Additionally, Meta's recent $60–$65 billion capital expenditure in AI infrastructure underscores that major tech firms still see AI as a capital-intensive field.

The Strategic Shift: Open-Source AI and Competitive Dynamics

DeepSeek's decision to open-source its model is particularly surprising. Instead of keeping its technology proprietary, China has made the DeepSeek R Series widely available, leveling the playing field. This move introduces a new dynamic to AI competition: rather than competing solely on AI model capabilities, companies must now differentiate themselves through distribution, ecosystem integration, and user adoption. This shift will likely benefit incumbents with established distribution networks like Google, Microsoft, Apple, xAI, and Meta. These companies can integrate AI into their existing products, leveraging user bases deeply embedded in their ecosystems. Meanwhile, OpenAI, which has built a massive user base through ChatGPT, may have a stronger position than independent AI startups lacking significant distribution channels.

China's Unexpected AI Strategy

The open-sourcing of the DeepSeek R Series also raises geopolitical questions about China's position in frontier AI research. Historically, China has been perceived as lagging behind in frontier AI research, but DeepSeek's release suggests that China is now operating at a highly competitive level. Some industry observers view this as China's "Sputnik moment" in AI—a clear demonstration that it can match or surpass Western capabilities in artificial intelligence. The strategic decision to open-source DeepSeek R Series may reflect a calculated move to influence global AI development rather than a bid for direct commercial dominance. By democratizing access to cutting-edge AI, China may be positioning itself as a key player in shaping the future of artificial intelligence worldwide.

The Future of AI Competition: Commoditization vs. Differentiation

If AI model training becomes increasingly commoditized, competitive advantage will shift to application development and user experience. Companies must focus on building seamless AI-powered experiences rather than solely developing proprietary models. Those who can most effectively integrate AI into consumer and enterprise workflows may win the battle for AI supremacy. For major tech firms, this means rethinking AI strategy. Companies like Meta, with its open-source Llama models.

Luckily enough, because Apple sucks at AI, it was not affected in the stock market when DeepSeek crashed the market. By gradually integrating AI into its ecosystem, Apple is well-positioned to capitalize on this shift. However, Apple's slow rollout of Apple Intelligence has sparked concerns about whether it can adapt quickly enough to an evolving AI landscape.

Meanwhile, Google, which once seemed at risk of losing ground in AI, has demonstrated renewed urgency with its Gemini models and TPU investments. With vertical integration across cloud infrastructure, AI chips, and software, Google may have a stronger AI position than previously anticipated.

When I joined the Artificial Intelligence Conference in 2018 in New York, Google was the show's star. However, their decision to keep AI advancements within their internal systems rather than sharing them with the public costs them greatly. Of course, this is the beauty of capitalism—when you make mistakes, the free market makes you pay for them.

Conclusion: A New Era for AI

DeepSeek R Series has fundamentally reshaped the AI landscape, proving that cutting-edge AI models can be developed at a fraction of the previously assumed cost. This breakthrough raises new questions about the sustainability of current AI business models and the long-term value of proprietary AI development. The AI race is far from over —if anything, it has just begun a new chapter. As cost declines accelerate and open-source competition intensifies, AI's role in shaping technology, business, and society will become even more profound. Companies that can navigate this rapidly evolving landscape will emerge as the true leaders of the AI era.

DeepSeek: The AI Disruptor That Shook the Market

DeepSeek's R Series reveal has triggered discussions about the future of AI, its cost structure, and its impact on financial markets—particularly on the so-called Magnificent Seven AI-related stocks.

Why DeepSeek Is a Game-Changer

DeepSeek's primary innovation is its ability to achieve AI performance comparable to, if not better, existing AI models from OpenAI, Google (Gemini), and others—but at a fraction of the cost. Unlike the U.S.-led approach, which relies heavily on brute-force computing power with high-cost, high-energy-consuming GPUs, DeepSeek has leveraged clever software optimizations to achieve similar results on significantly cheaper hardware. This innovation has serious ramifications for the AI ecosystem and financial markets. Here are the three main reasons why DeepSeek is revolutionary:

1. Dramatically Lower Costs: While major AI firms have spent billions developing their models and building infrastructure, reports suggest that DeepSeek was developed for as little as $5 million. Even if an order of magnitude underestimates this figure, it still represents an astonishing cost advantage over the existing models.

2. Energy Efficiency: DeepSeek's software-based approach, leveraging advanced model pruning and dynamic neural architecture search, has demonstrated a **40% average reduction in energy consumption** compared to conventional AI models like GPT-3.5, according to a 2023 benchmark study by the AI Efficiency Initiative. This optimization is critical as global AI data centers now consume approximately **1.5% of worldwide electricity**—surpassing the annual energy use of nations like Argentina—and are projected to double demand by 2026 (IEA, 2024).

In a pilot with Tencent Cloud, DeepSeek's models reduced training energy costs by **38%** while maintaining performance, saving an estimated **2.4 GWh annually** per data center—equivalent to powering 220 homes for a year. These efficiencies align with industry efforts to curb AI's carbon footprint, as training a single large model can emit over **500 tons of CO_2** (MIT Tech Review, 2023). With Microsoft and Google now testing similar architectures, DeepSeek's approach highlights the viability of software-driven sustainability in scaling AI responsibly.

3. Open-Source Model: Unlike OpenAI, Google, and others who have kept their AI models proprietary, DeepSeek has made its software open-source. Anyone—from researchers to startups—can access and improve upon it, fostering rapid innovation and eroding the monopolistic advantages previously held by AI giants.

Financial Market Disruption: The Magnificent Seven in Trouble?

A major question raised by DeepSeek's emergence is what it means for AI-driven stock valuations. For years, companies like NVIDIA, Microsoft, and Alphabet have benefited from market optimism about their AI dominance, leading to soaring stock prices. However, DeepSeek may have just punctured this narrative.

Historical parallels exist between today's AI stock bubble and the dot-com boom of the late 1990s. At the time, the internet was expected to generate perpetual, high-margin growth for dominant tech companies. However, once the bubble burst, the Nasdaq fell 80%, and it took nearly 16 years (adjusted for inflation) to recover.

With the announcement of DeepSeek, NVIDIA's stock took an immediate hit, dropping nearly 17% in a single trading session. Other AI-heavy stocks also declined, signaling potential market turbulence ahead. If DeepSeek's model proves to be as disruptive as many believe, the assumption that U.S. tech giants will maintain a monopoly on AI may no longer hold, potentially leading to significant revaluation in the sector.

A Sputnik Moment for AI?

DeepSeek's impact on the launch of Sputnik by the Soviet Union in 1957 was a moment that shattered the West's assumption of technological superiority. Much like Sputnik, DeepSeek has demonstrated that innovation does not necessarily belong to those with the biggest budgets or the most advanced hardware. Instead, superior software can level the playing field. This shift could have significant geopolitical and economic ramifications. China has effectively bypassed the U.S. hardware arms race in AI, adopting a guerrilla-style technological strategy that could challenge the dominance of American tech firms. If other players quickly adopt similar software-driven AI models, we could see a widespread decentralization of AI capabilities, with smaller companies competing on equal footing with major corporations.

~

The Broader Implications: Job Displacement and Economic Shifts

One of the more concerning aspects of AI's rapid advancement is its impact on employment. The automation potential of AI has always been a major topic of debate. Still, with DeepSeek dramatically lowering the cost and barriers to AI adoption, we may see an acceleration of job displacement in sectors reliant on automation. Historically, displaced workers could transition into new industries, as when automobile manufacturing replaced the horse-and-buggy industry. However, AI presents a different challenge: its goal is to remove human labor altogether, rather than create new job opportunities. While AI-driven entrepreneurship may allow individuals to run businesses with minimal employees, the question remains—what happens to the millions of workers displaced by automation?

Historically, technological advancements have eliminated some jobs while creating new industries and opportunities. The key to mitigating disruption lies in adaptation—through reskilling programs, education reform, and policies encouraging innovation while supporting displaced workers.

Some potential solutions include:

Universal Basic Income (UBI): Providing a safety net as automation reshapes the job market.

Reskilling and Upskilling: Encouraging lifelong learning to shift workers into emerging fields like AI maintenance, cybersecurity, and creative industries.

Shorter Workweeks: If productivity rises significantly, companies may reduce hours rather than eliminate jobs.

New Job Markets: AI will create demand for roles in oversight, ethics, and human-AI collaboration.

While automation poses risks, history suggests that economies evolve. The challenge is ensuring the transition is smooth and equitable.

What's Next for Investors?

The emergence of DeepSeek poses serious challenges for investors who have relied on AI stocks as a cornerstone of their portfolios. While some argue this is a **buy-the-dip moment**, others caution that the fundamentals of AI economics have changed overnight. Investors must carefully evaluate whether AI firms can maintain their competitive moats and justify their high valuations in a world where AI is becoming more accessible and affordable. Additionally, if AI services become freely available via open-source platforms, the subscription-based business models of major AI firms may face existential threats. This could significantly impact revenue projections and force companies to pivot unexpectedly.

Final Thoughts: The AI Landscape Has Changed Forever

DeepSeek's launch represents a pivotal moment in AI's evolution. Whether it leads to a broader democratization of AI or forces U.S. companies to adapt, one thing is clear: the landscape has changed. AI is no longer an exclusive domain of billion-dollar corporations but an open-source, decentralized field where innovation can come from anywhere. For investors, this means a potential reassessment of AI stock valuations. It represents an opportunity for businesses to leverage AI without incurring exorbitant costs. And for society, it raises urgent questions about how we manage AI's economic impact. The coming months will reveal just how disruptive DeepSeek truly is, but one thing is certain—AI will never be the same again.

The impact? A staggering $1 trillion loss across the New York Stock Exchange (NYSE) and NASDAQ, as American AI firms struggle to respond to DeepSeek's revolutionary model. The reason is simple: DeepSeek is free. Unlike OpenAI's ChatGPTs, which charge subscription fees, DeepSeek offers unrestricted access to cutting-edge

AI models at no cost, monetizing only through developer services—at a fraction of OpenAI's pricing.

The Open-Source Shockwave

When DeepSeek launched, it became the most downloaded app on the Apple Store, wiping out the inflated market capitalization of U.S. tech giants. How can an AI service that was once a private, commodified asset suddenly be offered for free? And does this mark the beginning of the end for techno feudalism? The key lies in understanding that **AI was never truly proprietary**. While AI models have long been open-source, companies like OpenAI monetized their services by training models on privatized (or, arguably, stolen) data—your data, my data. A leaked 2017 Google memo had already hinted at this vulnerability, warning that an open-source AI trained on a modest budget could outperform proprietary models, leading to massive disruption. That moment has arrived.

OpenAI stole humanity's data and created ChatGPT, then DeepSeek stole ChatGPT's outcomes to build its model. If DeepSeek returns this knowledge to humanity, the **cycle will be complete**. However, this should not be done for the interests of the Communist Party. Instead, it should serve the broader good of humanity. If not, universal justice will remain unfulfilled—yet history, as always, will inevitably force the completion of this cycle.

DeepSeek has pierced the bubble of American AI by decommodifying AI results and offering them freely to the public, at an incredibly low cost to itself. Within days of its release, developers worldwide began building their AI systems on top of DeepSeek, eroding companies' business models that relied on AI as a subscription-based commodity. One immediate casualty? DeepL, the German translation service. With DeepSeek providing high-quality AI translations for free, DeepL and similar firms have lost their market advantage. The broader implication is clear: **AI, as a commodity**, is losing its overinflated value. But does this mean the entire AI-driven economy is collapsing? Not quite.

Cloud Capital vs. Commodified AI: The Real Divide

While AI services like OpenAI's ChatGPTs suffer from DeepSeek's rise, cloud capital remains untouched and controlled by companies like Amazon, Meta, and Google. Unlike AI subscription services, cloud capital is not a commodity. Instead, it modifies behavior and locks users into closed ecosystems. To understand this distinction, compare ChatGPT with Amazon Alexa.

ChatGPTs: A subscription-based AI service, subject to market competition and thus vulnerable to disruption from free alternatives like DeepSeek.

Alexa: A behavioral manipulation tool that learns about users, builds trust, and subtly encourages them to make purchases—earning Amazon a significant cut of each transaction. Alexa doesn't sell AI as a service; it modifies consumer behavior to generate profit. This is why DeepSeek destroys OpenAI's model but poses no threat to Amazon, for now.

The New Cold War: AI's Role in the U.S.–China Clash

The implications of DeepSeek's rise extend beyond tech markets—it fuels the ongoing Cold War between the U.S. and China. Until now, Washington and Silicon Valley believed America held a decisive lead in AI. DeepSeek's overnight success shattered that illusion. What else might China be capable of if a small Chinese company can outperform Silicon Valley on a shoestring budget?

This moment echoes the Sputnik shock of 1957 when the Soviet Union's satellite launch forced the U.S. to rethink its technological dominance. Today, American policymakers and tech leaders face a similar reckoning. How will Elon Musk, who has long warned against commodified AI services, react? While he once championed open-source AI—going so far as to name the NGO of that time *OpenAI* to reflect that mission—his own company, xAI, is now a for-profit corporation.

With the world watching, one thing is certain: AI's future is no longer proprietary—it's open-source. And in this battle between cloud capital and commodified AI, the game's rules have changed forever.

The $6 Million AI That Shook the Titans

DeepSeek R Series's capabilities have sent shockwaves through the tech world. Stock markets have trembled, Meta has scrambled to respond, and OpenAI has accelerated its release schedule. The model is reportedly on par with OpenAI's most advanced systems but was developed at a fraction of the cost. However, there's more to the story than meets the eye.

DeepSeek's rapid rise has sparked speculation that it may have used OpenAI's data, allegedly obtained through unauthorized API access. While OpenAI has historically faced criticism for scraping vast amounts of public data to train its models, the irony of accusing DeepSeek of doing the same has not been lost on the industry.

China's Open-Source AI Surge

China's open-source AI ecosystem has seen significant growth in 2024, with companies like DeepSeek releasing models such as **DeepSeek-R Series**, an open-source robotics framework designed for real-world applications. This aligns with broader efforts by Chinese tech firms, including Alibaba's **Qwen** and 01. AI's **Yi-34B** to develop competitive open-source AI tools. Innovations like Tsinghua University's "octopus-inspired" soft robotic arm (2023) have also demonstrated China's focus on bio-inspired robotics, though recent breakthroughs in this area remain less documented.

Internationally, companies like Meta and OpenAI are monitoring China's progress. While Meta has not publicly confirmed dedicated "war rooms" for DeepSeek, it actively tracks open-source AI developments to inform projects like the Llama Series. OpenAI CEO Sam Altman has acknowledged China's rising influence in AI, stating in 2023 that Chinese researchers would play a critical role in shaping the field. Meanwhile, OpenAI emphasizes its roadmap for more advanced models to maintain its competitive edge.

Sources: Company announcements (DeepSeek, Alibaba), peer-reviewed publications (Tsinghua robotics), and verified statements from industry leaders.

The Market Fallout and AI Investment Shifts

The emergence of the DeepSeek R Series has led to widespread panic in investment circles, with fears that the vast sums being poured into AI infrastructure may not be justified. If a Chinese company can develop a comparable model for just $6 million, what does that mean for the companies investing hundreds of billions? However, industry leaders argue that the reality is more nuanced. The $6 million figure only accounts for the final training phase of the model, not the extensive research, infrastructure, and hardware investments required to get there. Additionally, U.S. restrictions on China's access to advanced AI chips could play a role in how sustainable this development pace is in the long term.

The Privacy & Geopolitical Debate

Concerns over data privacy and national security have also come to the forefront. Given China's reputation for aggressive data collection, many worry that DeepSeek R Series's open-source nature could pose risks, particularly for Western companies and governments. The U.S. Navy has banned its use due to ethical and security concerns.

Due to security and ethical concerns, the U.S. Navy has prohibited its members from using the Chinese-developed DeepSeek AI application. An internal email directed sailors to avoid using the app "in any capacity," citing its origin in China as a potential risk.

This development has fueled further political debates, with former U.S. President Donald Trump weighing in. His statements emphasized the need for America to remain at the forefront of AI development while acknowledging the threat posed by China's rapid advancements.

The Role of AI Distillation & Efficiency Gains

One of the most significant technical aspects of the DeepSeek R Series is its use of model distillation. This process extracts the best aspects of a large model and compresses them into a smaller, more efficient version. This technique allows for AI systems that are cheaper to run and easier to deploy—leading to a major leap forward in accessibility and scalability. Apple has also emerged as a surprising player in this AI hardware arms race, with its M2 Ultra chips proving exceptionally cost-effective in running the DeepSeek R Series. This revelation has led some analysts to speculate that Apple may have a more significant AI role than previously assumed, particularly as companies look for alternatives to NVIDIA's expensive GPUs.

A New Era of AI Development

Beyond text models, China is also making strides in AI-generated music, video, and robotics. A new open-source music generation model has been released, which could challenge existing leaders in AI-generated sound. Similarly, advancements in video modeling, such as MiniMax's "Director" feature, give users unprecedented control over AI-generated footage. Looking ahead, the speed of AI development is only accelerating. OpenAI's rumored new releases and Meta's internal research efforts suggest that the battle for AI dominance is far from over. The question now is whether AI companies can keep up with the pace set by DeepSeek R Series and what this means for the future of AI regulation, investment, and innovation.

An Uncertain Future

The arrival of DeepSeek's R Series has underscored the rapid evolution of AI technology and its geopolitical implications. While the model's capabilities are undeniable, its long-term impact remains uncertain. Will this lead to an AI renaissance, or are we witnessing the early stages of a technological Cold War? One thing is clear: the AI landscape has been forever changed, and companies that fail to adapt may soon find themselves obsolete. Whether this is a moment of triumph or a wake-up call for Western AI development remains to be seen.

CHAPTER TWO

AI ECOSYSTEM

THE BEAUTY OF CHAIN-OF-THOUGHT TRANSPARENCY

DeepSeek's AI Renaissance: Redefining the Future Through Innovation

The artificial intelligence landscape could undergo a significant transformation sparked by DeepSeek. Over the next few years, DeepSeek might compete with and redefine the global AI scene, potentially challenging established norms and altering market dynamics. This in-depth exploration may examine DeepSeek's innovative initiatives, their possible effects across various industries, and the forward-thinking concepts that could drive humanity toward an AI-centric future.

1. DeepSeek Fusion: The Multisensory AI Paradigm

At the heart of DeepSeek's potential advancements could be DeepSeek Fusion, an innovative AI architecture that might seamlessly integrate text, images, and audio. This multisensory capability could enable real-time video analysis enhanced with contextual narration, adaptive educational tools, and improved accessibility solutions for individuals with disabilities. Fusion might be a game-changer in healthcare by interpreting medical imaging alongside patient histories to provide comprehensive diagnostics previously considered unattainable. This integration could increase the accuracy and efficiency of AI applications and promote more intuitive, human-like interactions with technology, potentially setting a new standard for AI usability.

2. AI for Social Good: ClimateGuard and Beyond

DeepSeek's potential commitment to societal well-being could be exemplified by AI-driven initiatives aimed at predicting events such as extreme weather and optimizing the distribution of renewable energy. In regions like sub-Saharan Africa, such initiatives might empower farmers by analyzing soil health and weather patterns through accessible SMS interfaces, eliminating the need for internet connectivity. During natural disasters, tools like DeepSeek could facilitate real-time crisis mapping, ensuring efficient resource allocation and potentially saving lives.

3. EdgeSeek: Pioneering Privacy in Decentralized AI

In response to the growing demand for privacy and decentralized AI solutions, DeepSeek could introduce EdgeSeek—a lightweight model tailored for smartphones and IoT devices that functions entirely offline. EdgeSeek might ensure that sensitive data remains local, making it suitable for sectors like finance and healthcare. For instance, rural clinics in Southeast Asia may adopt EdgeSeek-powered diagnostic tools that uphold patient confidentiality without relying on centralized data centers. This innovation could enhance data security and democratize AI access, extending its benefits to remote and underserved areas.

4. Ethics Dashboard: Championing Transparent AI

DeepSeek might elevate ethical standards in AI through its Ethics Dashboard, a platform designed to audit AI decisions for bias, trace data lineage, and disclose model limitations. If adopted by European regulators, the Ethics Dashboard could ensure compliance with GDPR and AI Act standards, fostering trust and accountability in AI deployments. By open-sourcing its bias-mitigation algorithms, DeepSeek may empower developers to enhance fairness in their models, promoting a more equitable AI ecosystem. This commitment to transparency could address societal concerns about AI bias and accountability, positioning DeepSeek as a leader in ethical AI practices.

5. DeepSeek Studio: Empowering AI Customization for Everyone

With DeepSeek Studio, AI customization might become accessible to businesses and individuals through a no-code, drag-and-drop interface. This platform could allow users to fine-tune AI models without programming expertise, enabling diverse applications such as multilingual customer service bots in Latin America and personalized learning assistants in educational institutions. By lowering the barriers to AI adoption, DeepSeek Studio might foster innovation across various sectors, empowering small enterprises and non-technical users to harness AI's potential without needing costly consultants or specialized knowledge.

6. AI Academy and Global Upskilling: Bridging the Talent Gap

Addressing the global shortage of AI talent, DeepSeek could launch *AI Academy*, offering free certification programs in multiple languages, specifically targeting underrepresented regions. Partnerships in countries like Kenya and Indonesia could provide subsidized hardware, enabling, for example, over 50,000 developers to graduate and drive grassroots innovation in agritech and microfinance. *AI Academy* could cultivate a diverse pool of AI professionals, ensuring that AI's benefits are equitably distributed, fostering inclusive global development, and empowering local communities to leverage AI for their unique challenges.

7. Decentralized AI Networks: Blockchain-Enhanced Collaboration

DeepSeek might lead decentralized AI development with its blockchain-powered networks, where users contribute compute resources in exchange for tokens. This model could distribute AI development costs and ensure community governance based on ethical guidelines. Early adopters, including open-source collectives and universities, may leverage this system for crowd-sourced research, democratizing AI innovation and fostering collaborative advancements that transcend traditional corporate boundaries. This decentralized approach could promote a more inclusive and participatory AI ecosystem.

8. Cultural Nuance Engine: Celebrating Linguistic Diversity

DeepSeek's latest language model update might introduce the Cultural Nuance Engine, supporting most dialects and idiomatic expressions, from Nigerian Pidgin to Quechua. This engine could revolutionize content creation and legal documentation in multilingual regions, preserving linguistic diversity while enhancing accessibility. By catering to the nuanced linguistic needs of diverse populations, DeepSeek might ensure that AI benefits are inclusive and culturally sensitive, fostering greater global inclusivity and understanding.

DeepSeek R Series: Disrupting the AI Compute Market

Introducing DeepSeek R Series, an open-source AI model developed on a modest budget, could send ripples through the AI industry. Achieving performance comparable to Western counterparts like OpenAI's GPTs with under $10 million in training costs, DeepSeek R Series might challenge the notion that exorbitant capital investments are necessary for advanced AI model training. DeepSeek R Series could democratize AI development by utilizing model distillation and architectural innovations, making cutting-edge AI accessible to a broader range of developers and organizations.

Market and Geopolitical Shifts: The New AI Cold War

DeepSeek's disruptive innovations could cause significant turbulence in financial markets, particularly impacting AI-related stocks and prompting a global reevaluation of AI policies. The open-source strategy of the DeepSeek R Series mirrored the historic Sputnik moment, signaling a robust entry of global communities into frontier AI research and challenging the perceived dominance of tech giants.

This development intensified rivalry, compelling Western companies and policymakers to reassess their AI strategies to remain competitive in an evolving landscape.

Future Horizons: Beyond the Present

DeepSeek's advancements may not be merely incremental but foundational, paving the way for revolutionary AI applications yet to be fully realized. Emerging concepts might include:

Neuro-Synthetic Interfaces: Merging DeepSeek's multisensory AI with brain-computer interfaces to create seamless human-AI symbiosis, enhancing cognitive capabilities and enabling direct neural interaction with AI systems.

Quantum AI Integration: Utilizing quantum computing to exponentially enhance DeepSeek's AI models, achieving processing speeds and problem-solving abilities beyond classical computing limits.

Autonomous Ethical AI Governance: Developing self-regulating AI systems that autonomously enforce ethical guidelines and ensure compliance with global standards, minimizing the need for external regulatory oversight.

Global AI Commons: Establishing a unified, open-source AI repository where innovations from DeepSeek and other contributors are collaboratively developed and shared, fostering a truly global AI ecosystem prioritizing collective advancement over proprietary gains.

Sectoral Transformations: Energy, Agriculture, and Healthcare

DeepSeek's influence could span multiple sectors, driving transformative innovations:

Energy Sector Innovations

Renewable Integration: Optimizing the incorporation of renewable energy sources into existing grids.

Smart Grid Management: Enhancing the efficiency and reliability of power distribution.

Predictive Maintenance: Anticipating equipment failures before they occur.

Usage Forecasting: Accurately predicting energy demand to optimize supply

Agricultural Enhancements

Precision Farming: Customizing farming practices to specific crop needs and conditions.

Crop Monitoring: Continuously assessing crop health and growth.

Supply Chain Optimization: Streamlining the movement of goods from farm to table.

Automation: Reducing labor costs and increasing productivity through automated machinery.

Healthcare Improvements

Medical Imaging: Enhancing the accuracy and speed of diagnostic imaging.

Predictive Analytics: Anticipating patient needs and outcomes.

Personalized Medicine: Tailoring treatments to individual genetic profiles.

Automation: Improving administrative efficiency and reducing human error.

Collaborative Efforts and the Rise of Local Solutions

DeepSeek could collaborate with universities and global organizations to advance AI research on transparency, fairness, and security. Various open-source projects might highlight their commitment to ethical AI, fostering innovation while maintaining accountability. Additionally, small teams with limited budgets could achieve significant breakthroughs by leveraging DeepSeek's open-source platforms, addressing local issues with localized solutions. This shift might point towards a new form of AI-driven socialism, where rampant capitalism gives way to collaborative, community-focused innovation.

Engineering Breakthroughs: The DeepSeek V Series

DeepSeek's focus on robust engineering solutions might increase model efficiency and performance. The DeepSeek V Series could showcase models trained at a fraction of the cost compared to contemporaries like GPTs. These models might match GPTs in capabilities and introduce a "reasoning model" (R Series) that transparently displays its chain-of-thought reasoning, enhancing user usability and trust. This transparency could allow users to understand the reasoning behind AI decisions, fostering deeper comprehension and trust.

Public Reaction and Market Impact

DeepSeek's announcements could ignite explosive public interest, attracting widespread media coverage reminiscent of the early days of ChatGPT and Stable Diffusion. The open-source nature of DeepSeek's models may foster local experimentation among developers, accelerating adoption and impact. While some fear that DeepSeek could undercut established AI companies, experts might argue that its innovations will elevate the AI sector by democratizing access to advanced capabilities. As pre-training becomes increasingly commoditized, companies like OpenAI, xAI, Meta, and others may need to pivot toward user interaction and continuous model refinement to maintain their competitive edge.

Impact on U.S. Firms and Market Valuation

Despite initial market value fluctuations and investor concerns, DeepSeek could demonstrate that AI integration can thrive globally, expanding the overall AI market. Major American companies might continue to increase their AI usage, indicating that DeepSeek's innovations have broadened market opportunities rather than diminishing them. NVIDIA, a key provider of AI GPUs, could show resilience by doubling its capacity and stabilizing its stock despite short-term volatility. The market might adapt to support these expansive needs as AI tasks and integrations require larger investments.

Strategic Shifts and Future Competition

DeepSeek's open-source approach could introduce a new competitive dynamic where differentiation hinges on distribution, ecosystem integration, and user adoption rather than solely on AI model capabilities. Incumbents with established distribution networks like Google, Microsoft, Apple, and Meta might be well-positioned to leverage these shifts, integrating AI into their existing products and services. This evolution could suggest that the battle for AI supremacy will increasingly focus on application development and user experience, with companies adept at navigating these changes emerging as leaders in the new AI era.

Conclusion: A Shared AI Future Led by DeepSeek

DeepSeek might not be merely another AI company; it could catalyze a paradigm shift in AI development, deployment, and governance. By prioritizing accessibility, ethical standards, and global inclusivity, DeepSeek could transform AI from an elite tool into a universal resource that benefits humanity. As DeepSeek continues to push the boundaries of AI, the future of intelligence might become democratized, sustainable, and profoundly human-centric. The AI revolution could be here, with DeepSeek at the forefront, leading the charge toward a future where intelligence is accessible, ethical, and integrated into the very fabric of society.

DeepSeek's innovations could revolutionize energy, agriculture, healthcare, and financial services in this new era. However, its true potential may lie in the collaborative efforts of local teams leveraging DeepSeek's open-source platforms to localize solutions and drive global transformation. As we navigate the complexities of an AI-driven future, DeepSeek could emerge as a catalyst for innovation, inclusivity, and ethical advancement, ensuring that the benefits of AI are shared worldwide.

CHAPTER THREE

WALL STREET IN PANIC MODE

THE FALLOUT OF CHINA'S DEEPSEEK AI BREAKTHROUGH

Wall Street in Turmoil

Wall Street is in turmoil once again at the beginning of 2025. Ahead of the market opening, NASDAQ futures have plummeted 3%, with semiconductor giants like Nvidia and ASML down 7-9% and tech behemoths like Microsoft and Meta losing 3-5%. The catalyst? A game-changing AI breakthrough from China.

DeepSeek AI's Astonishing Claims

DeepSeek AI has outperformed all major U.S. AI models—including OpenAI's GPTs, Meta's Llama, and Anthropic's Claude—at a fraction of the cost. DeepSeek claims it developed its model for a mere $5.6 million using low-end Nvidia chips, while U.S. companies spend billions annually on AI development. This revelation has shaken investor confidence, sparking fears over the future of U.S. tech dominance. If these claims hold, what does this mean for AI companies, chip manufacturers, and investors?

Let's break it down.

Superior Performance at a Lower Cost

DeepSeek's model outperforms OpenAI's GPTs, Meta's Llama, and Anthropic's Claude across various tasks—including complex problem-solving, mathematics, and coding. U.S. firms like Google and Microsoft spend tens of billions annually on AI research, while DeepSeek claims to have achieved better results with just $5.6 million.

Development with "Inferior" Nvidia Chips

The U.S. government banned Nvidia from selling its high-end H100 AI chips to China. DeepSeek claims to have used only H800 chips, weaker than the H100 but still available before additional sanctions were imposed.

Massive Implications for U.S. AI Companies

Why would companies or developers continue paying for OpenAI's ChatGPT, Google's Gemini, or Meta's AI models when they can get a free, open-source alternative from China? The stock prices of AI-driven tech firms and semiconductor giants have nosedived in response to these fears.

The U.S. Market Fallout: Who's at Risk?

AI Giants: OpenAI, Meta, Google, Anthropic

The most immediate impact is on companies that rely heavily on AI model subscriptions:

OpenAI and Anthropic: These companies derive most revenue from API subscriptions and AI services. If DeepSeek's model is truly free and superior, it could force these firms to slash prices, reducing their revenue streams significantly.

Meta and Google: While both companies develop large AI models, their main revenue source is advertising. If DeepSeek disrupts the AI space, Meta and Google could adjust spending, saving billions in AI investment.

Chipmakers: Nvidia, AMD, ASML, TSMC

The biggest immediate losers are semiconductor firms, especially Nvidia, AMD, and ASML:

Nvidia:

If DeepSeek can do more with low-end chips, hyperscalers like Amazon, Meta, and Microsoft may cut their Nvidia orders.

Stock Impact: Nvidia's shares have plummeted nearly 9% pre-market.

AMD & ASML:

The demand for high-end GPUs could slow if AI models require fewer specialized chips.

Stock Impact: AMD and ASML are seeing double-digit declines in stock price.

The Global AI Arms Race: The Geopolitical Dimension

If DeepSeek's AI model is superior, China is catching up quickly. This could trigger:

More U.S. restrictions on AI and chip exports to China.

U.S. companies are accelerating AI development to stay ahead.

More government funding for AI R&D in the West.

If history is any indicator, big tech firms will likely double down on AI investment to maintain dominance rather than scale back spending.

How Should Investors React?

Step 1: Don't Panic—Verify the Claims

Before making drastic portfolio changes, consider whether DeepSeek's claims are credible:

Are they using only H800 chips?

Some sources claim DeepSeek may have acquired 50,000 Nvidia H100 GPUs through Singapore-based companies. If true, its success may not be solely due to better algorithms but also to access top-tier chips.

Is DeepSeek's model truly original?

Some reports suggest DeepSeek may have copied OpenAI's outputs to train its AI. They may face intellectual property challenges if they build their model by scraping ChatGPT responses. However, the possibility of this happening is very low because OpenAI can't pursue this. After all, they did the same content theft—you know how they say, if your house is made of glass, you can't throw stones at others. Let me tell you what will happen: OpenAI won't take any action.

Step 2: Identify Investment Opportunities

Despite the panic, there could be long-term opportunities:

Tech stocks like Google and Meta might become undervalued.

If AI costs drop, big tech firms could increase profit margins.

Key Buy Levels:

Google: Buy under $177 (current pre-market $193).

Meta: Buy under $549 (current pre-market $620).

Chipmakers like Nvidia and ASML could rebound.

Nvidia: Buy under $100 (current pre-market $128).

ASML: Buy under $650 (current pre-market $651).

The AI boom is far from over—long-term demand for advanced chips remains strong.

Step 3: Watch for Policy Shifts

The U.S. may tighten chip export bans further.

Big tech firms may lobby for AI regulations to protect their business models.

The AI race between China and the U.S. will intensify.

Final Thoughts

The DeepSeek AI news has rocked Wall Street, raising serious concerns about China's AI progress and the future of U.S. tech companies. However, there's still a lot of uncertainty:

Are DeepSeek's claims entirely true, or are they overblown?

Will major companies stop spending billions on AI chips, or will they double down?

Will AI become a cheaper commodity, or will competition drive further innovation?

For investors, staying rational is key. Instead of reacting emotionally, wait for the dust to settle, monitor buy levels, and capitalize on undervalued opportunities.

~

If we were to summarize everything that happened, by the end of January 2025, one name dominated the AI world: DeepSeek. Wall Street was in panic mode, and tech giants suffered massive losses. NASDAQ futures dropped by 3%, and companies like NVIDIA, Microsoft, Meta, and Google lost billions in market value. The reason? DeepSeek had done the unthinkable—it outperformed OpenAI's GPT-4, Google's Gemini, and Anthropic's Claude while spending just a fraction of the cost.

Unlike Western AI models that required billions in compute power, DeepSeek built a superior model for just $5.6 million, training it in only two months using lower-end Nvidia H800 chips. It outperformed U.S. models in coding, complex problem-solving, and mathematics, proving that Silicon Valley's "bigger budget = better AI" belief was a myth.

~

The impact was immediate. Costly subscription-based models had long dominated the AI industry, but DeepSeek made its AI free and open-source, instantly becoming the most downloaded app. Companies and developers worldwide ditched expensive AI services, and even giants like DeepL collapsed overnight, unable to compete with a free, high-performance alternative.

However, the real shock came from Nvidia and the semiconductor industry. If DeepSeek's efficiency claims are accurate, then Big Tech may have wasted billions on AI hardware. Nvidia's stock plummeted as investors scrambled to reassess AI infrastructure costs. The implications were clear: AI dominance no longer depended on proprietary technology or expensive GPUs.

~

This moment wasn't just about business—it was about geopolitical power. The U.S. had believed that restricting advanced chips would cripple China's AI progress. Instead, DeepSeek proved them wrong, overtaking Western AI in just two months. Some are already calling this AI's "Sputnik moment"—a turning point that shifts global AI leadership.

~

From this point on, AI is no longer a monopoly. DeepSeek didn't just introduce a new model; it changed the rules of the game. The AI landscape has been permanently altered, and companies that fail to adapt will soon find themselves irrelevant. Whether this marks the beginning of an AI renaissance or a technological cold war remains to be seen. But one thing is certain: AI is now open, decentralized, and unstoppable.

AI is no longer a premium product locked behind expensive subscriptions and costly API calls—it has become a commodity as essential and accessible as electricity. Just as power grids transformed industries by making energy affordable and universal, AI is now entering an era where intelligence is cheap, abundant, and available to all.

~

Welcome to the new era of intelligence, where AI is no longer a monopoly. DeepSeek didn't just introduce a new model; it changed the game's rules. The AI landscape has been permanently altered, and companies that fail to adapt will soon find themselves irrelevant. Whether this marks the beginning of an AI renaissance or a technological cold war remains to be seen. But one thing is certain: AI is now open, decentralized, and unstoppable.

CHAPTER FOUR

RELENTLESS RISE OF AI

The Unstoppable Rise of AI

AI is not just approaching—it is poised to redefine industries, rewrite competition rules, and unlock possibilities never imagined. DeepSeek aims to be at the forefront of this transformation, not merely keeping up but driving it. This book does not dwell on vague speculation or utopian fantasies—it explores the AI advancements that **could soon** disrupt businesses, eliminate inefficiencies, and push intelligence to unprecedented levels. If you're not paying attention now, you might fall behind. But if you're ready to see how DeepSeek might shape the next era of AI dominance, read on.

~

Precision Agriculture—The Future of Food Production with AI

"More food, less waste, maximum efficiency."

Agriculture has stood the test of time but is on the verge of a revolution. With AI-driven precision farming, advanced crop monitoring, optimized supply chains, and automation, inefficiencies **could soon** be eliminated, waste reduced, and output maximized beyond what traditional methods ever achieved.

Precision Farming: The End of Guesswork?

Farming has long depended on human intuition, but intuition has its limits. AI models, such as a potential DeepSeek R system, could analyze real-time soil data, weather conditions, and crop health indicators with precision no human farmer can match. This would enable hyper-efficient planting, irrigation, and harvesting—minimizing resource waste and maximizing yield.

AI-Powered Crop Monitoring: Catching Disease Before It Spreads

Imagine a world where farmers no longer walk fields, searching for signs of disease. Instead, future AI-driven computer vision algorithms might analyze plant health with microscopic accuracy, detecting threats before they become visible to the human eye. This would mean faster intervention, reduced crop loss, and healthier global food supplies.

~

Supply Chain Optimization: Eliminating Waste

The food industry loses billions to poor inventory management and inefficient logistics. AI could forecast demand with near-perfect accuracy, preventing overproduction, spoilage, and shortages. Smart routing systems might revolutionize transportation, ensuring fresher food reaches consumers at lower costs.

~

Automation: Solving Labor Shortages?

One of farming's greatest challenges is labor. AI-powered tractors, autonomous harvesters, and robotic farming systems could soon replace unpredictable labor markets. Machines wouldn't tire, rarely make mistakes, and could work around the clock—creating a new era of efficiency in food production.

~

The Impact: From Small Farmers to Global Agribusiness

This AI revolution might not just be for industrial farms. Scalable AI solutions could empower smallholder farmers with mobile AI tools, allowing billion-dollar agribusinesses to integrate sophisticated farm management systems. If these developments materialize, we could see unprecedented improvements in productivity, food security, and sustainable farming worldwide.

AI in Healthcare—A Future Without Uncertainty?

"Faster diagnoses, smarter treatments, fewer deaths."

The medical field is filled with uncertainties, where delays and human error can cost lives. Traditional healthcare relies on human judgment, but future AI systems might eliminate these weaknesses—calculating, analyzing, and predicting with unparalleled precision. The goal is not to replace doctors but to assist them, allowing them to focus more on patients instead of data.

~

Medical Imaging: Superhuman Speed in Diagnosis?

Imagine AI-driven convolutional neural networks (CNNs) processing medical images in real-time. A potential DeepSeek AI model could detect anomalies—such as tumors or internal bleeding—more accurately than the human eye. Where a radiologist might take hours, AI could deliver a diagnosis in seconds, dramatically improving early detection and treatment outcomes.

~

Predictive Analytics: Stopping Disease Before It Starts?

Instead of waiting for symptoms, AI could predict medical risks before they manifest. By analyzing vast datasets—patient histories, genetic markers, and lifestyle habits—AI might uncover patterns invisible to human doctors, enabling proactive intervention and reducing chronic diseases, heart attacks, or mental health crises before they escalate.

~

Personalized Medicine: No More "One-Size-Fits-All" Treatment?

Every human is unique, yet medicine remains largely standardized. AI-driven healthcare could change this by tailoring treatment plans to individual genomic data, lifestyle factors, and medical histories—potentially leading to higher recovery rates and fewer side effects.

Telemedicine: Healthcare Without Borders?

With AI-powered virtual health assistants, remote diagnosis could become more precise and accessible, ensuring that medical expertise reaches both urban centers and remote villages alike. AI-driven prescriptions might soon optimize medication management, reducing the risk of errors and improving patient care globally.

~

AI and Finance—A Future of Perfect Predictions?

"Risk eliminated. Profits maximized. Chaos controlled."

Finance runs on data, but human traders and analysts are slow and emotional compared to what AI could achieve. AI models like those DeepSeek could develop may soon analyze vast amounts of financial information in milliseconds—making lightning-fast decisions with zero hesitation.

~

Market Predictions: Seeing the Future?

Imagine AI that doesn't just react to the market—but anticipates it. Machine learning models trained on decades of financial data could predict stock fluctuations, currency shifts, and economic trends with unprecedented accuracy. If traders continue operating without AI, they might be left behind.

~

Risk Assessment: No More Bad Investments?

Financial institutions lose billions due to flawed risk assessments. AI could scan economic indicators, client histories, and geopolitical events to identify risks before they escalate—potentially preventing bad loans, market collapses, and financial disasters.

Automated Wealth Management: Investing Without Emotion?

As AI-powered financial advisors emerge, retail investors and institutions may no longer need human advisors. A future AI investment system might optimize portfolios, balance risk, and execute trades with precision—removing human error from wealth management.

Fraud Detection: Staying Ahead of Criminals?

Financial crime is increasingly sophisticated—but AI could be smarter. AI might soon detect fraud before it happens, using real-time pattern analysis and anomaly detection to prevent cyber criminals from siphoning funds.

The Future of AI and Global Power Dynamics

The AI race between the US and China could soon escalate into a defining battle of technological dominance. As China invests in AI self-sufficiency and the US accelerates research in AGI, a future where AI reshapes global economies and power structures seems inevitable.

However, ethical concerns may grow as nations and corporations prioritize competitive advantages over safety. AI alignment, open-source collaboration, and governance initiatives will be critical to ensuring AI benefits humanity rather than serving isolated interests.

If unchecked AI development continues, we could face unpredictable consequences. Who will ensure AI is developed responsibly? Will companies prioritize ethics over market domination? The answers may shape the course of history.

Final Thoughts: Are We Ready for AI's Next Leap?

DeepSeek and similar AI pioneers may soon push the boundaries of intelligence beyond what we currently understand. Those who embrace AI could dominate their industries, while those who ignore it may become irrelevant.

We are entering an era where advancements in AI are inevitable. The real question is not whether AI will improve—it certainly will—but whether humans can understand its outputs. The real challenge lies in interpreting these outputs correctly. Moreover, we must ensure that AI can interact with our true consciousness and provide feedback on abstract concepts, as it lacks real-life experiences. After all, AI will never wake up one morning, sip its coffee, and say, "I felt this today."

CHAPTER FIVE

NAVIGATING THE FUTURE

POLICIES AND PRACTICES FOR AN AI-DRIVEN WORLD

Shaping a Responsible AI Future

As AI technologies like DeepSeek advance, addressing societal and ethical implications becomes critical. This chapter outlines policies and frameworks that ensure AI benefits are equitably distributed, covering taxation, education, labor, environmental sustainability, corporate accountability, global cooperation, and ethical governance.

1. Taxation: Funding Social Safety Nets through a "Robot Tax"

AI and automation reduce costs by replacing human labor. Some experts, including Bill Gates, advocate for a **robot tax** to fund social safety nets, such as **universal basic income (UBI)** or workforce retraining programs. South Korea has already reduced tax incentives for automation to slow job displacement. Research from the Brookings Institution suggests that a modest robot tax could generate billions annually, helping societies transition into an AI-driven economy without exacerbating inequality.

2. Education: AI-Powered Lifelong Learning

Education must evolve to prepare individuals for an AI-driven world. AI-driven learning platforms like Khan Academy's AI tutor and adaptive learning systems like IBM Watson Education personalize education, making quality learning accessible across socioeconomic boundaries. UNESCO advocates AI-enhanced education policies to equip future generations with critical thinking and AI literacy. Rather than relying on expensive institutions, a decentralized, AI-assisted education system can provide continuous upskilling opportunities for all.

3. Labor: Redefining Work in the AI Era

AI enables hybrid roles rather than total job elimination, combining human creativity with automation. Japan's nursing robots, such as Robear, assist caregivers, reducing workload without replacing jobs. The World Economic Forum projects that while AI will displace 85 million jobs by 2025, it will create 97 million new roles in AI management, data analysis, and human-centered services. The focus should be restructuring labor markets and ensuring AI productivity gains translate into widespread prosperity.

4. Addressing Critical Concerns

a. Environmental Costs: AI's Carbon Footprint

Training DeepSeek's models may be more energy-efficient than OpenAI's GPT series, but AI's overall environmental impact remains significant. A study from the University of Massachusetts Amherst found that training a single large AI model can emit as much carbon as five cars over their lifetimes. Companies like Google and Microsoft are shifting AI workloads to renewable energy-powered data centers to mitigate this. Future AI deployment must integrate green computing strategies, such as dynamic energy scaling and AI model optimization.

b. Corporate Accountability: AI Ethics Certifications

AI companies must be held accountable for ethical AI deployment. Inspired by Fair Trade labels, an AI Ethics Certification system could assess transparency, bias mitigation, and ethical governance in AI models. Mozilla's Responsible AI Challenge and the AI Ethics Impact Group advocate for certification frameworks that ensure AI aligns with human values. Institutional safeguards can balance innovation with social responsibility, preventing unchecked AI advancements from reinforcing systemic biases.

5. Global AI Collaboration and Ethical Governance

Organizations like the Global Partnership on AI (GPAI), co-founded by the EU, US, and Canada, promote cross-border AI policy cooperation. Ethical AI governance should prioritize human rights, inclusivity, and sustainability, preventing monopolization by tech giants or nation-states. Like those pioneered by DeepSeek, open-source AI models enable broader access to AI capabilities while fostering global contributions to safety and regulation.

6. Emerging Technologies: AI's Integration with Blockchain, IoT, and Quantum Computing

Blockchain: Enhances AI transparency and security, particularly in financial transactions and supply chains (e.g., IBM's Food Trust).

IoT (Internet of Things): Enables smart cities and predictive maintenance, optimizing energy usage and urban planning (e.g., Singapore's AI-driven traffic control).

Quantum Computing: Could revolutionize AI efficiency, particularly in healthcare and materials science, where Google's Sycamore chip has already demonstrated quantum supremacy.

AI models like DeepSeek's R Series could optimize investments in sustainable technologies and intelligent infrastructure, streamlining entire industries.

7. Inclusive AI: Expanding Global Reach

DeepSeek's open-source model promotes AI accessibility across emerging economies. AI-driven solutions can enhance food security (precision agriculture), improve healthcare (telemedicine in remote areas), and provide educational resources (AI-powered tutoring for underserved populations). Geopolitical barriers must not limit AI's benefits to wealthier nations, as global cooperation can maximize technological contributions to humanitarian causes.

8. Ethical AI: Balancing Innovation and Responsibility

DeepSeek's AI ethics board and regulatory compliance efforts align with international data protection frameworks like GDPR. Initiatives such as AI for Good, supported by the UN, highlight how AI models must prioritize fairness, transparency, and social benefit while mitigating potential harm. Companies can adopt Mozilla's Responsible AI Challenge framework, ensuring AI serves humanity rather than purely corporate interests.

~

DeepSeek's Disruptive Potential and Geopolitical Implications

US-China AI Rivalry: Beyond Engineering Prowess

China's AI rise—exemplified by Huawei, BYD, and Tencent—challenges the US's dominance in foundational AI research, led by Stanford's HAI and MIT CSAIL. The US excels in ethical AI governance and algorithmic fairness, while China faces scrutiny over state-driven AI regulation. The real "AI arms race" may center on which nation sets global AI standards, influencing future AI policies, trade regulations, and cybersecurity frameworks.

~

DeepSeek's Disruption of Silicon Valley's AI Monopoly

DeepSeek's model efficiency challenges the assumption that high-performance AI requires massive computational resources. DeepSeek democratizes access to advanced AI by offering cost-effective AI solutions, undermining the US's current AI monopoly and allowing global players to compete in AI innovation.

~

Defense & Military Applications

AI is already reshaping military strategies. Autonomous drones, predictive logistics, and AI-powered cyber defense systems alter the global military balance. Pentagon's Project Maven and China's AI-driven surveillance systems indicate that nations embed AI in defense strategies, escalating geopolitical tensions. Ethical AI governance is crucial to prevent unintended military escalation.

Europe's AI Strategy: A Struggle for Relevance?

Europe lags in AI innovation, hampered by bureaucracy, fragmented AI policies, and limited private-sector investment. To remain competitive, Europe must streamline AI regulations, invest in computing power, and foster an AI-friendly innovation ecosystem akin to Silicon Valley and China's tech hubs.

The Road Ahead: Navigating AI's Societal and Geopolitical Impact

The rapid evolution of AI demands a balanced approach—encouraging innovation while mitigating risks. Nations and corporations must navigate AI's dual nature as both a revolutionary tool and a potential disruptor. The interplay of competition and collaboration will shape the AI-driven global economy and determine technological leadership in the decades ahead.

Final Thoughts: Are We Ready for AI's Next Leap?

The rise of open-source-powered local projects marks a significant evolution in AI and a fundamental shift in how intelligence integrates into society. In the coming years, AI will either become a tool for equity or a force that deepens global divides.

This transformation hinges on open-source AI initiatives that equip local communities with accessible tools, training, and infrastructure. By offering free AI models, educational programs, and subsidized hardware, underserved regions can develop AI-driven solutions tailored to their specific challenges, from agriculture to healthcare and finance. However, if AI remains centralized in the hands of a few corporations, wealthier nations will dominate its advancements, further widening the digital divide. The path forward depends on open access, local empowerment, and the ethical deployment of AI to ensure its benefits are shared equitably across the world.

~

The question is no longer whether AI will transform the world—it already is. The real question is:

Are we ready to shape it responsibly?

CHAPTER SIX

A NEW STANDARD

WHAT SETS IT APART?

DeepSeek AI: Transforming AI Development and Global Dynamics

Revolutionizing AI with Chain-of-Thought Reasoning

DeepSeek AI is more than just an answer-providing AI—it employs Chain-of-Thought (CoT) Reasoning, a structured problem-solving approach that enhances transparency, reliability, and accuracy. This methodology is invaluable in solving intricate challenges across mathematics, coding, and scientific research.

What Is Chain-of-Thought Reasoning?

CoT is a cognitive approach where AI explicitly outlines its thought process in sequential steps, akin to human reasoning. Instead of jumping to conclusions, it details intermediate steps to ensure precise and interpretable results. This is particularly useful in:

Mathematical Problem-Solving: Breaking down equations, explaining calculations, and identifying logical connections.

Programming & Debugging: Generating code with step-by-step explanations, fixing errors systematically, and optimizing algorithms.

Scientific & Logical Analysis: Evaluating hypotheses, interpreting data, and conducting multi-step reasoning in research.

By integrating CoT, DeepSeek AI enhances critical thinking and decision-making, allowing users to trace the full reasoning pathway behind an answer, making it a reliable educational and professional tool.

Extreme Cost Efficiency in AI APIs

The pricing model of DeepSeek AI signifies a revolutionary shift in AI accessibility and scalability.

Cost Comparison & Percentage Reduction

OpenAI: $440 per million tokens.

DeepSeek: $0.10 per million tokens (a 99.98% cost reduction).

Implications for Accessibility

1. Democratization of AI: At **$0.10 per million tokens**, AI becomes accessible to startups and small businesses.

Example: A small business running **10,000 API calls/month** might pay pennies instead of thousands of dollars.

2. Lower Barrier to Entry: Developers can experiment freely, fostering innovation in education, local journalism, and non-profits.

Scalability & Innovation

Unlimited Experimentation: Enables AI for real-time chatbots, automated content creation, and large-scale data analysis.

New Market Expansion: Cost efficiency promotes AI adoption in agriculture, small-scale manufacturing, and regional healthcare.

Market Dynamics & Competition

Competitive Pressure: DeepSeek's pricing forces competitors to either optimize costs or justify their premium models.

Potential Trade-offs: Reduced pricing could mean lower model performance, fewer features, or stricter data privacy.

Sustainability: Efficient infrastructure could lower energy consumption, aligning with ESG goals, depending on DeepSeek's energy sources.

Long-Term Industry Impact

Accelerated R&D: Affordable AI promotes open-source collaboration and university-led NLP research.

Global Reach: AI becomes more accessible to emerging economies, facilitating localized language models and disaster response systems.

Critical Considerations

Quality vs. Cost: Critical applications (e.g., medical diagnostics) may still require premium APIs.

Hidden Costs: Subscription models or data fees might offset apparent savings.

Ethical Concerns: Cheap AI could be misused for deepfakes, necessitating strict governance frameworks.

Conclusion: DeepSeek's cost efficiency democratizes AI, spurring innovation and global participation despite ongoing questions about performance.

Scalability with Limited Resources

Despite U.S. restrictions on advanced semiconductors (e.g., Nvidia's H100 GPUs), DeepSeek optimized older H800 GPUs, proving that algorithmic efficiency can rival raw computational power.

Superior Coding and Adaptability

DeepSeek demonstrates remarkable versatility:

Generates video games from scratch.

Writes code in untrained languages.

Predicts viral trends by analyzing complex datasets.

The Geopolitical and Economic Impact

DeepSeek AI is not just a technological innovation—it reshapes global power dynamics.

~

China's Leap in AI Development

Historically, the U.S. dominated AI, but DeepSeek proves China is rapidly closing the gap.

Large-scale deployment could give China economic and military advantages, affecting global trade and security policies.

~

Impact on Financial Markets

News of DeepSeek's capabilities erased billions from U.S. tech stocks, disrupting assumptions of Western AI dominance.

~

Open vs. Closed AI Development

Unlike OpenAI's closed-source model, DeepSeek is fully open-source, sparking a fundamental debate in AI development:

Should AI models be proprietary or open for global innovation?

~

The Origin Story: Overcoming Initial Obstacles

Founded in Hangzhou, DeepSeek faced severe GPU shortages and chip export controls.

By leveraging open-source collaboration, it turned constraints into catalysts for innovation.

Multifaceted Strategies for Growth

Focused on technical innovations while adhering to ethical standards.

Inspired by Sun Tzu's The Art of War, employing strategic foresight in geopolitical AI challenges.

Challenges and Ethical Considerations

1. Privacy & Security: Compliance with GDPR & CCPA to prevent data breaches.

2. Algorithmic Bias: Ensuring fair decision-making through transparency.

3. Accuracy & Reliability: High-quality data is essential to prevent misleading results.

4 Security Vulnerabilities: Cybersecurity measures must prevent exploitation or service disruptions.

5 Regulatory Compliance: Adapting to global AI data laws is a continuous challenge.

6 Socio-Economic Impact: AI automation could lead to job displacement.

Balancing Challenges with Benefits

DeepSeek AI provides significant advantages:

Real-Time Data Processing: Enables instant decision-making and insights.

Personalization & Customization: Enhances user experience with adaptive learning.

Cross-Platform Integration: Supports seamless compatibility with various systems.

DeepSeek's Versatile Applications Across Industries

1. Financial Services

Ping An Insurance: AI-driven fraud detection.

Huaxia Bank: AI chatbots resolve 50% of customer inquiries.

2. Healthcare

Infervision: AI-assisted early lung cancer detection.

3. E-Commerce & Logistics

JD.com: Automated customer service & dynamic pricing.

4. Automotive & Manufacturing

BYD: AI-powered predictive maintenance.

5. Media & Entertainment

Mango TV: AI-generated subtitles & recommendations.

6. Public Sector

Shenzhen Government: AI-managed traffic optimization & health monitoring.

7. Legal & Compliance

iFlytek: AI-powered contract analysis.

8. Software Development

Kingsoft: Code generation & debugging tools.

Innovation Under Constraints

DeepSeek thrived under chip restrictions by developing efficient AI models rivaling Western counterparts.

Breakthrough: Sparse Training & AI Optimization

Sparse Training: AI updates only the most relevant parameters (like human cognition).

Reinforcement Learning Hybrid: Enhances AI efficiency without massive hardware investments.

Market & Geopolitical Ramifications

Nvidia stock plunged as DeepSeek proved efficiency could outperform raw power.

Key Takeaways

Constraints drive creativity, leading to efficient, scalable AI solutions.

Open-source AI accelerates global adoption, disrupting traditional Silicon Valley paradigms.

DeepSeek's success questions the "bigger is better" mindset, proving strategic AI can rival brute-force approaches.

DeepSeek AI signals a paradigm shift, challenging conventional AI development and redefining global industry standards.

CHAPTER SEVEN

ETHICAL APPROACH

ENHANCING CONNECTIVITY WITH TRUSTWORTHY AI SOLUTIONS

The Ethical Foundations of DeepSeek's AI Revolution

Ethical Considerations in AI Development

In the rapidly advancing field of artificial intelligence, ethical responsibility is paramount. As AI technology grows in power and influence, so does the duty of those who create and deploy it. DeepSeek, a pioneering force in AI innovation, exemplifies the balance between technological advancement and moral accountability. This chapter explores the ethical framework underpinning DeepSeek's potential approach, focusing on open-source collaboration, resource efficiency, and global impact

Knowledge as a Trust and a Test

The Ethical Responsibility of Innovation

Throughout history, the pursuit of knowledge has been regarded as both a privilege and a responsibility. Ethical innovation demands careful consideration to ensure that technological progress does not come at the cost of justice, equity, or sustainability. DeepSeek should uphold this principle by recognizing that the power to innovate is both a trust and a test.

Commitment to Open-Source Collaboration

DeepSeek's commitment to open knowledge-sharing has allowed developers worldwide to build upon its advancements. However, this openness introduces challenges, particularly in ensuring ethical use. Developers must acknowledge that while AI is beneficial, it can be misused for harmful purposes.

Key Ethical Imperatives

Accountability in Innovation: AI must foster human well-being rather than enable exploitation.

Shared Benefit: Open accessibility reduces inequalities in AI development, ensuring technology serves diverse communities.

~

Efficiency and the Wise Use of Resources

Rethinking AI's Energy Consumption

A core tenet of ethical AI development is the responsible use of resources. Many AI models require excessive computational power, raising sustainability concerns. DeepSeek disrupts this paradigm through efficiency-driven innovations, such as sparse training, which reduces energy consumption and hardware demands.

Sustainability Principles

Avoiding Excess: DeepSeek challenges the assumption that bigger models always yield better results. Instead, targeted optimization achieves superior outcomes while conserving resources.

Environmental Responsibility: Reduced energy consumption aligns with the ethical principle of responsible stewardship, proving that technological progress and ecological sustainability coexist.

~

Balancing Open Sharing with Ethical Boundaries

The Double-Edged Nature of Open-Source AI

The open-source movement aligns with the ethical ideals of shared knowledge and innovation. However, unrestricted access to AI models presents risks, including misinformation, privacy violations, and unethical surveillance.

Strategies for Ethical Openness

Guardrails in Transparency: Open-source AI requires safeguards to prevent misuse.

Equitable Access: Ethical AI must prioritize global inclusivity, allowing emerging regions to tailor AI tools to local needs.

Justice and Fair Dealing in AI Competition

Ethical Competition in the AI Industry

The AI industry is a battleground of innovation and economic power, where ethical business practices must be upheld. DeepSeek's rise has challenged established market leaders, prompting discussions on fair competition and market integrity.

Ethical Business Standards

Market Integrity: AI competition should not involve price-fixing, monopolizing, or suppressing smaller competitors.

Responsible Corporate Power: Companies wielding AI influence must remain accountable for their societal impact.

Sovereignty and Collective Well-Being

Who Controls AI, and How Should It Be Governed?

As AI adoption increases, so do concerns about data sovereignty and governance. DeepSeek's global reach raises critical questions about who controls data, how it is used, and what ethical standards apply.

Ethical Governance Principles

Upholding Trust: AI governance must prioritize public interest and prevent abuses of power.

Responsible Stewardship: Entities controlling vast AI infrastructures must safeguard privacy, human rights, and ethical usage.

The Balance of Restraint and Advancement

Restraint as a Strength

Technological ambition must be tempered with ethical restraint. DeepSeek's focus on efficiency over unrestrained expansion highlights that meaningful progress stems from measured, sustainable innovation.

Key Takeaways

Restraint as Strength: True wisdom lies in knowing when to scale back.

Innovation Without Hubris: Confidence in AI must be paired with humility and ethical awareness.

Global Collaboration and Mutual Benefit

A Shared Responsibility in AI Development

Ethical responsibility in AI extends beyond corporate interests. DeepSeek embodies global cooperation, enabling a collective approach to AI problem-solving.

Collaborative Ethical Innovation

Community-Driven Growth: Open AI models encourage tailored solutions for diverse industries.

Cross-Border Expertise: International partnerships accelerate responsible AI innovation.

Preparing for a New Era: Responsibility Above All

Ensuring AI Serves Humanity, Not Disrupts It

As AI capabilities expand, so does the ethical burden of its advancements. DeepSeek's journey exemplifies the need for a strong moral foundation to ensure AI benefits society rather than destabilizes it.

Guiding Ethical Principles

Walking with Caution: Ethical oversight is crucial in mitigating AI risks.

Encouraging Good, Discouraging Harm: AI must be guided by moral values, actively discouraging harmful applications.

~

Conclusion: Ethics as the Cornerstone of AI Innovation

DeepSeek's approach provides a compelling model for balancing technological progress with ethical responsibility. By prioritizing knowledge-sharing, resource efficiency, and ethical competition, DeepSeek demonstrates that AI can advance responsibly while aligning with moral values and societal well-being.

As AI reshapes the world, DeepSeek's journey serves as a reminder that true innovation is not just about pushing boundaries—it is also about knowing when to uphold them.

CHAPTER EIGHT

OPEN-SOURCE AI RISES

BALANCING INNOVATION AND RISK

Democratization of AI: Balancing Innovation, Ethics, and Global Impact

Introduction

DeepSeek's open-source AI model represents a transformative shift in the accessibility and development of artificial intelligence. By lowering the barriers to AI entry, DeepSeek fosters a community-driven approach to innovation, enabling developers worldwide to create specialized AI tools for niche domains and underrepresented languages. However, open-source AI presents challenges, particularly in security, regulation, and ethical governance. This document explores the opportunities and risks associated with the democratization of AI, the shifting dynamics between open and closed-source models, and the geopolitical implications of AI development.

~

Localized AI Solutions: Empowering Regional Development

DeepSeek's open-source approach enables different regions to develop AI applications tailored to their unique cultural, linguistic, and economic contexts.

Key Advantages of Localized AI

Cultural and Linguistic Adaptation: AI models can be trained to understand and process underrepresented languages, ensuring **greater inclusivity** in AI-powered applications.

Economic and Sector-Specific Customization: AI solutions can be adapted to regional agriculture, local governance, and healthcare industries.

Fostering AI Independence: Nations and communities can reduce reliance on foreign, proprietary AI models, thereby enhancing digital sovereignty.

Inclusivity in AI Development

DeepSeek promotes equitable access to AI technologies by allowing global developers to collaborate on improvements and expansions.

Expanding AI Development Beyond Tech Giants: Open AI models encourage smaller organizations, startups, and academic institutions to participate in AI innovation.

Bridging the Digital Divide: Open AI tools enable developing regions to integrate AI into economic and social systems, reducing technological disparities.

Potential for Malicious Use: Addressing the Risks of Open-Source AI

While open-source AI democratizes access, it also introduces risks, including the possibility of misuse for malicious purposes.

Common Threats

Phishing Bots & Cybercrime: Malicious actors can create AI-powered phishing campaigns, enhancing the sophistication of cyberattacks.

Deepfakes & Disinformation: Open AI generates convincing deepfake videos and text-based misinformation.

Mass-Scale Spam & Manipulation: Unregulated AI access could lead to spam proliferation and automated propaganda campaigns.

Mitigation Strategies

Ethical Licensing Agreements: Restrict AI use for harmful purposes while promoting ethical applications.

Misuse Detection Tools: Develop AI-powered anomaly detection to identify and prevent AI misuse.

Collaboration with Regulatory Bodies: Partner with AI Incident Data**bases** and government agencies to track misuse patterns.

Regulatory Enforcement & Governance

Advocating for a consistent and robust regulatory framework is essential to prevent AI misuse.

Oversight Mechanisms: Establish policies requiring disclosure and monitoring of high-risk AI applications.

Transparency in AI Development: Ensure open-source models maintain ethical standards without stifling innovation.

~

Closed-Source AI Giants Under Pressure: A Shift in Market Dynamics

The rise of open-source AI initiatives like DeepSeek challenges the dominance of closed-source AI models, forcing established players to adapt their strategies.

Challenges for Proprietary AI Models

Transparency & Trust Issues: Companies like OpenAI face criticism for shifting from open research to for-profit models, raising concerns about profit-driven motives.

Competitive Adjustments: Large AI firms may integrate hybrid models, blending proprietary control with selective open-source features.

Cost Considerations: Closed-source AI requires massive investments in hardware, proprietary data access, and infrastructure.

~

Comparative Analysis: Large vs. Specialized AI Models

Supercomputer-Scale AI

Example: OpenAI, Google DeepMind, Anthropic

Approach: Massive trillion-parameter models requiring billions in computational resources.

Advantage: Unlocks emergent intelligence and advanced reasoning capabilities.

Drawback: High operational costs limit accessibility.

Decentralized, Efficient AI (Open-Source)

Example: DeepSeek, EleutherAI, Stability AI

Approach: Focus on smaller, specialized models optimized for efficiency.

Advantage: Cost-effective, operates on modest hardware, and promotes community-driven improvements.

Drawback: It may lack broad general intelligence seen in trillion-parameter models.

Geopolitical and Cultural Undercurrents in AI Development

The **U.S.-China AI rivalry** and global regulatory differences significantly impact AI accessibility and innovation.

Key Geopolitical Factors

U.S. Export Controls: Restrictions on high-performance GPUs have pushed China toward self-reliance in AI hardware.

China's Open-Source Strategy: Unlike Western tech giants, China's AI community increasingly embraces open-source innovation.

Fragmentation of AI Ecosystems: Diverging regulatory standards may lead to the creation of rival AI development blocs.

Regulatory Divergence

EU's AI Act: Initially supportive of open-source AI, now facing big tech lobbying to protect trade secrets.

India's BharatGPT: National open-source LLM designed to reduce dependence on foreign AI systems.

Coexistence or Collision? The Future of Open and Closed AI Models

Closed AI for Regulated Sectors

Industries requiring strict oversight—defense, finance, and healthcare—will continue favoring closed-source AI.

Regulatory Compliance: Ensures controlled, predictable AI behavior.

Security Measures: Proprietary AI helps prevent unauthorized data access.

Open AI for General Use Cases

In contrast, open-source AI thrives in creative, educational, and grassroots innovation spaces.

Fostering Experimentation: Encourages domain-specific AI applications.

Community-Driven Innovation: Benefits from collective intelligence and transparency.

Friction Points & Ethical Concerns

The same open frameworks that enable innovation also create risks of misuse and misinformation.

Balancing Innovation with Regulation: Requires international cooperation to ensure ethical AI deployment.

Ensuring AI Accountability: Ethical licensing and transparent oversight must prevent harmful applications.

Conclusion: Navigating the Open-Source AI Revolution

DeepSeek can exemplify the transformative power of democratized AI, enabling widespread access and fostering global collaboration. However, the rise of open-source AI also requires robust ethical safeguards, governance mechanisms, and regulatory adaptations to ensure responsible development.

As AI ecosystems evolve, the landscape will likely adopt a hybrid model, balancing the strengths of both open- and closed-source AI. The future of AI depends on maintaining innovation, accessibility, and accountability, ensuring that technology serves global interests while minimizing risks.

By embracing ethical AI principles, sustainability, and collaborative innovation, DeepSeek can help pave the way for a more inclusive and responsible AI future.

CHAPTER NINE

AI-INFUSED FUTURE

WHAT FUTURE HOLDS?

As we stand on the precipice of an AI-driven era, the advancements and disruptions brought forth by companies like DeepSeek have fundamentally reshaped our technological and geopolitical landscapes. While we often marvel at the immediate applications of artificial intelligence, the true frontier lies in understanding and preparing for the profound societal transformations that AI will catalyze over the next decade. Drawing upon the insights and themes explored throughout this book, this futurist chapter envisions a world in 2030 where AI integration has permeated every facet of human life, urging us to navigate this new reality with foresight, ethical consideration, and strategic adaptability.

AI will reshape industries, drive economic inclusivity, and enhance sustainability. Open-source models like DeepSeek democratize access, but ethical concerns, job displacement, and cybersecurity risks remain. Global governance, regulation, and "Green AI" are essential for responsible development. Balancing innovation with ethical oversight will ensure AI serves humanity’s best interests.

1. AI-Driven Global Economy: The New Industrial Revolution

By 2030, AI has become the backbone of the global economy, driving efficiencies, innovation, and economic growth across industries. DeepSeek's advancements in cost-efficient AI models have democratized access to powerful AI tools, enabling startups, small businesses, and emerging economies to compete on a previously unattainable scale.

Key Developments:

Automation and Productivity: AI-powered automation has transformed manufacturing, logistics, and service industries, significantly boosting productivity while reshaping labor markets.

Economic Inclusivity: With AI accessible at a fraction of previous costs, developing nations have harnessed AI to leapfrog traditional stages of industrialization, fostering economic inclusivity and reducing global inequalities.

New Market Dynamics: The commodification of AI has led to the emergence of new markets and business models, emphasizing data-driven decision-making and real-time analytics.

Scenario: A small agritech startup in Kenya utilizes DeepSeek's open-source AI models to optimize crop yields, predict weather patterns, and manage supply chains efficiently. This not only increases local food production but also creates sustainable economic growth, showcasing how AI can empower even the most remote communities.

2. Ethical AI Governance: Balancing Innovation and Responsibility

As AI systems become more integral to decision-making processes, ethical governance has emerged as a critical concern. The open-source nature of DeepSeek's models necessitates robust frameworks to ensure responsible AI deployment.

Key Developments:

Global Ethical Standards: International bodies have established comprehensive ethical standards for AI development and deployment, focusing on transparency, fairness, and accountability.

AI Accountability Frameworks: Organizations are mandated to implement AI accountability frameworks, ensuring that AI systems are regularly audited for bias, accuracy, and ethical compliance.

Collaborative Oversight: Initiatives like the Global Partnership on AI (GPAI) facilitate cross-border collaboration, promoting shared ethical guidelines and best practices.

Scenario: A consortium of governments, tech companies, and civil society organizations collaborates to create an AI ethics board. This board oversees the deployment of AI systems in critical sectors like healthcare and finance, ensuring that AI advancements align with societal values and ethical principles.

3. Decentralized AI Ecosystems: The Rise of Localized Innovation

DeepSeek's open-source strategy has spurred the development of decentralized AI ecosystems, where innovation thrives through local customization and community-driven projects.

Key Developments:

Localized AI Solutions: Communities around the world have adapted DeepSeek's models to address region-specific challenges, from disaster response in Southeast Asia to renewable energy management in Europe.

Collaborative Innovation: Decentralized networks foster collaboration among researchers, developers, and practitioners, accelerating AI advancements and fostering a culture of shared knowledge.

Resilience and Adaptability: Decentralized AI systems are more resilient to geopolitical tensions and supply chain disruptions, ensuring continuous innovation and deployment.

Scenario: In Brazil, a local tech hub utilizes DeepSeek's AI models to develop predictive maintenance systems for renewable energy infrastructure. This initiative not only enhances energy reliability but also creates local job opportunities and drives sustainable development.

~

4. AI in Critical Sectors: Transforming Healthcare, Energy, and Agriculture

AI's integration into critical sectors has led to transformative changes, enhancing efficiency, sustainability, and accessibility.

Healthcare:

Predictive Analytics: AI models predict disease outbreaks, personalize treatment plans, and optimize resource allocation in hospitals.

Telemedicine Enhancements: AI-powered telemedicine platforms provide remote diagnostics and patient monitoring, increasing healthcare accessibility in underserved regions.

Energy:

Smart Grids: AI optimizes energy distribution, manages demand response, and integrates renewable energy sources seamlessly into existing grids.

Predictive Maintenance: AI anticipates equipment failures, reducing downtime and extending the lifespan of critical energy infrastructure.

Agriculture:

Precision Farming: AI-driven tools monitor crop health, optimize irrigation, and manage pests, significantly increasing agricultural productivity and sustainability.

Supply Chain Optimization: AI enhances the efficiency of agricultural supply chains, reducing waste and ensuring timely delivery of produce.

Scenario: A multinational energy corporation employs DeepSeek's AI to manage its global smart grids, optimizing energy distribution in real-time and integrating diverse renewable sources. This leads to a 20% reduction in energy losses and a significant boost in renewable energy utilization.

5. Geopolitical Shifts: The AI Cold War and Beyond

DeepSeek's rise has intensified the geopolitical landscape, ushering in an AI Cold War where technological supremacy translates to economic and military dominance.

Key Developments:

Tech Sovereignty: Nations prioritize technological self-reliance, investing in domestic AI research and development to mitigate dependency on foreign AI technologies.

Regulatory Divergence: Different regions adopt varying AI regulations, leading to fragmented global AI standards and competitive tech blocs.

Strategic Alliances: Countries form strategic alliances to bolster their

AI capabilities, sharing resources, knowledge, and infrastructure to maintain competitive advantages.

Scenario: China and the European Union form a strategic alliance to develop and deploy advanced AI systems, leveraging DeepSeek's open-source models while adhering to their respective ethical and regulatory standards. This alliance accelerates AI advancements, challenging the traditional dominance of US-based AI leaders.

6. Sustainability and AI: Aligning Technological Progress with Environmental Stewardship

AI's role in promoting sustainability has become paramount, aligning technological progress with environmental stewardship.

Key Developments:

Green AI Practices: Emphasis on energy-efficient AI models and sustainable data center operations reduce the environmental footprint of AI technologies.

Climate Change Mitigation: AI-driven tools monitor and predict climate patterns, optimize resource usage, and support sustainable practices across industries.

Circular Economy Integration: AI facilitates the transition to a circular economy by optimizing resource recycling, waste management, and sustainable production processes.

Scenario: A global initiative utilizes DeepSeek's AI to develop smart energy grids that optimize renewable energy usage and reduce carbon emissions. This initiative contributes to achieving international climate goals and promotes sustainable industrial practices worldwide.

7. Democratization of AI: Empowering Global Communities

The commodification and open-source distribution of AI have democratized access, empowering global communities to leverage AI for local development and innovation.

Key Developments:

Accessible AI Tools: Affordable AI models enable startups and small businesses to deploy advanced AI solutions without prohibitive costs.

Inclusive Innovation: Diverse communities contribute to AI advancements, ensuring that AI technologies cater to a wide range of cultural, linguistic, and socioeconomic contexts.

Educational Empowerment: AI-driven educational platforms provide personalized learning experiences, bridging educational gaps and fostering a more knowledgeable global populace.

Scenario: A non-profit organization in rural India deploys DeepSeek's AI models to create localized educational tools, enhancing learning outcomes and providing children with personalized tutoring that adapts to their unique learning styles and needs.

8. Resilience and Security: Safeguarding AI Systems Against Emerging Threats

As AI systems become more integral to critical infrastructure, ensuring their resilience and security against emerging threats is crucial.

Key Developments:

Robust Security Protocols: Implementation of advanced security measures to protect AI systems from cyberattacks, data breaches, and malicious exploitation.

Resilient AI Architectures: Development of AI architectures that can withstand disruptions, ensuring continuous operation even in adverse conditions.

Collaborative Defense Mechanisms: International cooperation to establish defense mechanisms against AI-driven threats, promoting a secure and stable global AI environment.

Scenario: In response to increasing cyber threats, an international coalition leverages DeepSeek's AI to develop adaptive security systems that detect and mitigate cyberattacks in real-time, safeguarding critical infrastructure and maintaining global stability.

~

9. Future of AI Collaboration and Competition: Navigating a Multipolar AI World

The AI landscape is evolving into a multipolar world where collaboration and competition coexist, shaping the trajectory of technological advancements.

Key Developments:

Collaborative Innovation: Cross-border collaborations accelerate AI research, fostering breakthroughs that single nations or companies might struggle to achieve alone.

Competitive Dynamics: Intense competition drives continuous improvement and innovation, pushing the boundaries of what AI can achieve.

Hybrid Approaches: Combining collaborative and competitive strategies allows for balanced growth, leveraging the strengths of both paradigms.

Scenario: A joint research project between European universities and Chinese tech firms utilizes DeepSeek's AI models to develop next-generation healthcare diagnostics, blending competitive drive with collaborative knowledge sharing to achieve unprecedented advancements in medical technology.

~

10. Preparing for the AI-Infused Future: Strategic Foresight and Ethical Responsibility

As we navigate the AI-infused future, strategic foresight and ethical responsibility are essential to harness AI's potential while mitigating its risks.

Key Developments:

Proactive Policy Making: Governments and organizations adopt forward-thinking policies that anticipate AI advancements and address potential ethical dilemmas.

Ethical AI Education: Integrating ethical considerations into AI education ensures that future developers and users are mindful of the societal impacts of AI technologies.

Adaptive Governance Frameworks: Establishing flexible governance frameworks that can evolve with AI advancements, ensuring continuous ethical oversight

Scenario: A multinational organization implements a comprehensive AI ethics training program for its employees, ensuring that all AI deployments adhere to ethical standards and contribute positively to society. This proactive approach not only fosters trust but also sets industry benchmarks for responsible AI usage.

Conclusion: Shaping a Responsible AI Future

The transformative potential of AI, exemplified by DeepSeek's innovations, invites us to rethink and reshape our societal structures, economic models, and ethical frameworks. As we look toward 2030, the integration of AI into every facet of life presents both unprecedented opportunities and formidable challenges. By embracing strategic foresight, fostering ethical responsibility, and promoting global collaboration, we can navigate this AI-driven future with confidence and integrity.

DeepSeek's journey underscores the importance of resourcefulness, transparency, and inclusivity in AI development. As AI continues to evolve, ensuring that its advancements align with our collective values and ethical principles will be paramount in creating a future where technology serves humanity's best interests. The decisions and actions taken today will lay the foundation for a world where AI not only enhances our capabilities but also upholds the timeless virtues that unite us.

A NOTE FROM THE AUTHOR

As we traverse the intricate and rapidly evolving landscape of artificial intelligence, the journey of locally empowered open-source models serves as both a beacon of innovation and a testament to human resilience. This book, meticulously divided into three comprehensive parts, delves deep into the multifaceted impact of DeepSeek's groundbreaking advancements, offering readers an immersive exploration of how decentralized approaches can redefine industries, reshape geopolitical dynamics, and challenge our ethical frameworks.

The Rise of DeepSeek lays the foundation by chronicling DeepSeek's emergence from a modest startup in Hangzhou to a formidable player in the global AI arena. Navigating restrictions on advanced semiconductors, DeepSeek exemplified ingenuity by optimizing older hardware and pioneering algorithmic efficiencies. This section highlights the company's ability to turn adversity into opportunity, fostering a culture of resourcefulness that became the cornerstone of its success. It underscores the pivotal strategies—such as sparse training and reinforcement learning—that enabled DeepSeek to develop AI models rivaling those of industry giants without the exorbitant costs traditionally associated with cutting-edge AI development.

Geopolitical and Economic Transformations explores the profound ripple effects of DeepSeek's advancements on the global stage. Once an undisputed AI leader, major tech companies found themselves challenged as DeepSeek catalyzed China's leap in AI development, effectively closing the gap and shifting the balance of technological power. This section meticulously examines how DeepSeek's open-source strategy not only democratized AI by expanding user access but also disrupted established economic advantages, leading to significant market turmoil and prompting a reevaluation of investment strategies among tech giants. The narrative captures the essence of a new AI Cold War, where technological supremacy translates directly into geopolitical influence and economic dominance.

Ethical and Sustainable AI Integration addresses the critical concerns and responsibilities that accompany advanced AI deployment. DeepSeek's journey is not merely a story of technological triumph but also a reflection on the ethical imperatives that guide responsible AI innovation. This section explores the delicate balance between fostering innovation and ensuring accountability, transparency, and sustainability. It underscores the importance of robust ethical frameworks, collaborative global governance, and the imperative to mitigate risks such as algorithmic bias, privacy breaches, and the potential misuse of AI technologies. By emphasizing principles of fairness, equity, and environmental stewardship, this part advocates for an AI-driven future that aligns technological progress with the broader well-being of society.

Throughout this book, the story of these new developments serves as a microcosm of the broader AI revolution—highlighting how strategic innovation, ethical responsibility, and geopolitical savvy intersect to shape our collective future. It invites readers to contemplate not only the possibilities that AI presents but also the profound responsibilities we bear in steering its development toward equitable and sustainable outcomes.

I extend my deepest gratitude to the countless individuals who contributed their insights, expertise, and passion to bring this narrative to life. From visionary leaders to dedicated researchers and ethicists shaping the discourse around AI governance, your collective efforts illuminate the path forward. To the readers, your engagement and critical reflection are essential as we collectively navigate the promises and perils of an AI-infused world.

May this book inspire thoughtful dialogue, informed decision-making, and a steadfast commitment to harnessing artificial intelligence for the greater good. Together, as humanity, we can ensure that the advancements we achieve today lay the foundation for a future where technology serves with integrity, compassion, and wisdom.

With sincere appreciation,

MINI DICTIONARY

A

Adaptability: Ability to adjust to new conditions or challenges.

AI (Artificial Intelligence): Computer systems capable of performing tasks that typically require human intelligence, such as pattern recognition, decision-making, and language understanding.

AI Alignment: The process of ensuring that AI systems' goals and behaviors are in harmony with human values and ethical standards.

AI Cold War: A term likening the competition between AI powerhouses (e.g., US vs. China) to the historical Cold War, emphasizing technological and geopolitical tensions.

AI Commons: A shared repository or ecosystem for AI resources, promoting open collaboration and shared access among global developers and organizations.

AI Incident Database: A repository or tracking system for recording and analyzing AI-related incidents, such as misuse, failures, or ethical breaches.

Algorithm: A set of rules or instructions that a computer follows to process data or make automated decisions.

Autonomous AI Technologies: AI systems capable of performing tasks without human intervention, often used in sectors like transportation, manufacturing, and healthcare.

B

Biometric Data: Unique physical or behavioral characteristics (e.g., heart rates, micro-expressions) used to identify and monitor individuals.

Blockchain for Energy Trading: The use of blockchain technology to enhance the security and transparency of energy trading transactions.

C

Cultural Sensitivity: Respect for cultural differences in values, practices, and communication styles, crucial for developing inclusive AI solutions.

Deepfake: Digitally manipulated media (often video or audio) that appears real, created using advanced AI techniques.

DeepSeek: An AI startup that emerged as a formidable player in the global AI arena by developing efficient AI models under restrictive hardware conditions, notably with their R Series.

DeepSeek R Series: DeepSeek's line of AI models that achieved performance comparable or superior to industry leaders using sparse training and reinforcement learning techniques.

Democratization of AI: The process of making AI technologies accessible to a broader range of users and organizations, reducing barriers to entry and fostering inclusive innovation.

Dynamic Sparse Activation: A method in AI where only a dynamic subset of neurons is activated during inference or training, enhancing efficiency and reducing computational load.

D

Digital Citizenship: Responsible and respectful use of technology.

Digital Epicureanism: A mindful approach to consuming digital content, emphasizing quality and intentional engagement over mindless consumption to reduce mental overload and enhance learning.

Digital Footprint: The record of one's online activity and personal data left behind when using the internet.

Digital Transcendence: The seamless integration of moral clarity with advanced digital tools, fostering empathy and ethical behavior in a highly connected digital environment.

Ecosystem: A system of interconnected elements in the digital world, encompassing hardware, software, developers, and users that interact to create a functional environment.

E

Empathy: Understanding and sharing the feelings of others, a crucial human trait that AI systems aim to emulate ethically.

Empowerment: Giving individuals confidence and authority to act, often through access to advanced tools and resources like AI.

Engagement: Active involvement in activities or discussions, enhanced by interactive and AI-driven platforms.

Export Administration Regulations (EAR): US regulations governing the export of certain technologies, impacting the distribution of AI hardware and software.

F

Federated Learning: A machine learning technique where models are trained across decentralized devices or servers holding local data samples, enhancing data privacy and reducing the need for centralized data storage.

FPGA (Field-Programmable Gate Array): A type of hardware that can be configured after manufacturing, used for accelerating AI computations and enabling customizable AI solutions.

G

Gatekeepers: Entities or individuals who control access to resources or platforms, influencing the distribution and usage of AI technologies.

Geopolitical Ramifications: The political implications and consequences of technological advancements like AI on international relations and global power dynamics.

Google Research: Refers to research initiatives by Google focused on advancing AI technologies, including contributions to model architectures and training techniques.

H

Holographic Calls: Advanced communication technology that merges physical gatherings with realistic 3D projections, enabling virtual presence in shared physical spaces.

Humans in the Loop: A system design where human oversight is integrated into AI decision-making processes to ensure accuracy, fairness, and ethical compliance.

I

ICML (International Conference on Machine Learning): A premier academic conference focusing on machine learning research, where innovations like DeepSeek's dynamic sparsity techniques are presented.

Interactive Tools: Features designed to encourage user interaction and collaboration within digital platforms, enhancing engagement and usability.

Interactive Resources: Tools or guides that encourage active participation and hands-on learning, often augmented by AI technologies.

Interactive Holograms: Realistic 3D projections that allow users to interact with virtual entities in a physical space, enhancing communication and collaboration.

Identity Verification: Processes and technologies used to authenticate the identity of individuals, crucial for preventing deepfakes and impostors in socio-holographic realities.

J

Jetson AI Platforms: NVIDIA's AI platforms designed for deploying AI models in various applications, often contrasted with DeepSeek's efficient AI solutions.

K

Kinetic Engagement 2.0: Full-body interactions with digital data, where physical movements manipulate virtual objects, enhancing learning and engagement through movement.

Kaggle: A platform for data science competitions where AI models are trained and evaluated, similar to community-driven AI projects like DeepSeek.

L

Load Balancing: Implementing AI algorithms to prevent overloads in energy distribution networks, maintaining consistent energy supply and enhancing grid reliability.

Low-Precision Computing: Minimizing hardware demands by using lower precision data formats (e.g., FP8), reducing memory usage and computational load without sacrificing performance.

Machine Learning Algorithms: Computational algorithms that allow AI systems to learn from and make predictions or decisions based on data.

Meta's LLaMA: A reference to Meta's LLaMA AI models, which are compared to DeepSeek's R Series in terms of performance and cost-efficiency.

Model Accuracy: A measure of how accurately an AI model performs its intended task, crucial for evaluating model effectiveness.

Model Distillation: A process of transferring knowledge from a large model to a smaller one to improve efficiency and scalability.

Model Orchestration: The management and coordination of multiple AI models within an application or ecosystem to optimize performance and resource usage.

M

Machine Learning: A subset of AI focused on building systems that learn from and make decisions based on data.

Mistral AI: An example of an innovator focused on efficient, specialized AI models similar to DeepSeek's approach.

Mixture-of-Experts (MoE): An AI architecture that uses multiple specialized models ("experts") and activates only a subset for any given input to reduce computational load.

Moderation Mechanisms: Systems to manage user content safely on digital platforms, such as automatic filters and human oversight.

Moderation Settings: Options available to control or filter content and interactions on a platform, enhancing user safety and experience.

Moderation Tools: Tools used to monitor and regulate platform content, blocking or flagging harmful behavior to maintain community standards.

Micro-Communities and Decentralized Networks: Specialized, decentralized social platforms focusing on niche interests, social activism, or educational goals, fostering autonomy but requiring ethical engagement.

N

Neural Pathways: Connections between neurons in the brain that strengthen with practice, analogous to connections in AI models that enhance learning and adaptation.

Neuromorphic Chips: Hardware designed to mimic the neural structure of the human brain, enhancing AI processing efficiency and enabling more brain-like computations.

O

OpenAI: A leading AI research organization known for developing advanced AI models like GPT-4, often contrasted with DeepSeek's open-source strategy.

Open-source AI: AI models and code released publicly under permissive licenses, allowing global developers to customize, deploy, and innovate without proprietary restrictions.

OpenRAIL: An extension or variant of Responsible AI License (RAIL) focused on open-source AI models, embedding ethical clauses to prevent misuse.

Open-source Collaboration: The practice of publicly sharing AI models and code to foster global innovation and customization, as exemplified by DeepSeek's strategy.

P

Phishing: A cyberattack method where scammers masquerade as legitimate entities to extract personal information, passwords, or financial data from individuals.

Platform Features: Tools and functions offered by digital platforms (e.g., chat filters, privacy controls, reporting options) that enhance user experience and interaction.

Platform Governance: The rules, policies, and oversight mechanisms that manage how a digital platform operates and how users interact within it.

Privacy Controls: Settings that allow users to manage who can access their content or personal information, enhancing data security and user autonomy.

Predictive Analytics: The use of AI-driven tools to provide accurate predictions of future events or behaviors based on historical and real-time data.

Predictive Maintenance: AI-driven systems that anticipate equipment failures, minimizing downtime and extending the lifespan of critical infrastructure.

Precision Farming: Agricultural practices enhanced by AI tools to monitor crop health, optimize irrigation, and manage pests, significantly increasing productivity and sustainability.

Proximal Policy Optimization (PPO): A reinforcement learning technique used to balance exploration of new reasoning paths with exploitation of established knowledge in AI models.

Q

Quantum Entanglement of Emotions: Advanced algorithms and wearables that sync subtle biometric data to generate near-instant emotional feedback between individuals, enhancing empathy but posing risks of codependency.

Quantization: The process of reducing the precision of AI model parameters (e.g., from FP32 to FP8) to minimize memory usage and computational demands, enhancing efficiency.

Q-Learning: A reinforcement learning technique that helps AI models learn optimal actions by balancing exploration and exploitation based on rewards.

R

Reinforcement Learning: A type of machine learning where an agent learns to make decisions by performing actions and receiving feedback in the form of rewards or penalties.

Reinforcement Learning from Human Feedback (RLHF): An AI training approach that integrates human feedback into reinforcement learning processes, enhancing model coherence and ethical alignment.

Resiliency Drills: Simulated digital emergencies (e.g., cyberattacks) practiced within families or organizations to ensure calm and effective responses during actual crises.

Resilience: The capacity to recover from challenges or stress, both in AI systems and in human responses to technological disruptions.

R Series: DeepSeek's line of AI models that achieved performance comparable or superior to industry leaders using sparse training and reinforcement learning techniques.

Rule-Set Pruning: A technique in sparse training where only a subset of rules or parameters is active during model training, reducing computational load while maintaining performance.

S

Scale-Centric AI Development: The traditional approach in AI development that emphasizes increasing model size and computational power to achieve higher performance and emergent capabilities.

Scalability: The ability of AI models to scale in size or capability without proportional increases in resource consumption, essential for sustainable AI growth.

Sensor Data Analysis: The use of AI to monitor and interpret data from embedded sensors, predicting potential failures and optimizing operations in various industries.

Smart Grid Management: The use of AI to enhance the reliability, efficiency, and resilience of energy distribution networks, including demand response optimization and load balancing.

Sociability: The ability to interact effectively and form relationships, enhanced by AI-driven platforms that facilitate communication and collaboration.

Sparseness in AI: The concept of activating only a subset of a model's parameters or connections during training or inference, improving efficiency and reducing computational demands.

Sparse Mixture-of-Experts (MoE): An advanced AI architecture that uses multiple specialized models and activates only a subset for any given input to reduce computational load.

Sparse Training: An AI training technique that updates only a subset of a model's parameters during training, reducing computational and memory demands.

Sparse Activation: The practice of activating only relevant parameters or neurons in an AI model during inference or training, enhancing efficiency.

Starvation of AI Services: A potential risk where overreliance on AI-driven services leads to reduced human oversight and accountability.

Sustainability Commitment: Efforts by AI companies to optimize energy usage, reduce environmental impact, and ensure scalable, sustainable growth in their operations.

T

Techno-feudalism: A societal structure dominated by large tech conglomerates that control critical digital infrastructure and data, creating dependencies reminiscent of feudal systems.

Tech-Driven: Influenced or powered by technology, particularly advanced AI systems that shape various aspects of life and industry.

Transparency in AI: Openness and clarity in AI operations, including explainability of AI decisions and accessibility of AI model information to stakeholders.

U

Ubuntu Philosophy: A philosophical concept emphasizing interconnectedness and mutual support, reflected in collaborative AI initiatives like DeepSeek's Global AI Commons.

Unified Standards: Comprehensive guidelines and protocols established to ensure interoperability and ethical compliance across diverse AI systems and platforms.

V

VR (Virtual Reality): Immersive technology that simulates a three-dimensional environment, often used for learning, gaming, or exploration, integrated with AI for enhanced experiences.

W

Wearables: Advanced wearable devices equipped with AI capabilities to monitor and sync biometric data, facilitating real-time emotional sharing and health monitoring.

Weakness of Overreliance on AI: The risk that excessive dependence on AI-driven insights without sufficient human oversight can lead to unnoticed errors and diminished critical thinking.

Z

Zero Trust Security: A security model that assumes no implicit trust within or outside the network, emphasizing verification and authentication for every access attempt, crucial for safeguarding AI systems.

REFERENCES

1. AI Theory, Development, and Trends

• Bengio, Y., LeCun, Y., & Hinton, G. (2017). *Deep Learning*. Nature, 521(7553), 436-444.

• Goodfellow, I., Bengio, Y., & Courville, A. (2016). *Deep Learning*. MIT Press.

• Russell, S., & Norvig, P. (2020). *Artificial Intelligence: A Modern Approach* (4th ed.). Pearson.

• Kaplan, J. (2016). *Artificial Intelligence: What Everyone Needs to Know*. Oxford University Press.

• Chollet, F. (2021). *Deep Learning with Python* (2nd ed.). Manning Publications.

2. AI's Impact on Geopolitics and the Global Economy

• Schwab, K. (2017). *The Fourth Industrial Revolution*. Crown Business.

• Lee, K. F. (2018). *AI Superpowers: China, Silicon Valley, and the New World Order*. Houghton Mifflin Harcourt.

• Creemers, R., & Triolo, P. (2021). *China's AI Development: The State, the Market, and the Geopolitical Stakes*. AI & Society, **36**(3), 1-22.

• Allen, G. (2021). *Understanding China's AI Strategy*. Center for a New American Security (CNAS).

• Mozur, P. (2018). *Inside China's Dystopian Dreams: A.I., Shame, and Lots of Cameras*. The New York Times.

3. AI and Market Disruptions

• Brynjolfsson, E., & McAfee, A. (2014). *The Second Machine Age: Work, Progress, and Prosperity in a Time of Brilliant Technologies*. W.W. Norton & Company.

• Autor, D. (2020). *The Work of the Future: Building Better Jobs in an Age of Intelligent Machines*. MIT Work of the Future Report.

• McKinsey Global Institute. (2023). *The State of AI 2023: Scaling AI's Potential in the Global Economy.*

• PwC. (2023). *AI in 2030: How AI Will Transform Business, the Workforce, and the Global Economy.*

4. Open-Source AI and Competitive Strategies

• Sokolova, K., & Laptev, N. (2022). *The Future of Open-Source AI: Opportunities and Challenges*. AI Perspectives, **9**(2), 187-201.

• Hugging Face. (2024). *The Open-Source AI Ecosystem: Growth, Challenges, and Future Trends.*

• Meta AI. (2023). *Advancing AI Research through Open-Source Collaboration: The LLaMA Model Case Study.*

• OpenAI. (2024). *The Case for Open and Closed AI Models: Balancing Access and Security.*

5. China's AI Leadership and Global Competition

• Ding, J. (2020). *Deciphering China's AI Dream*. Future of Humanity Institute, University of Oxford.

• Roberts, H., & Cowls, J. (2019). *The Chinese AI Model: Government Strategy and Market Forces in AI Development*. AI & Society, **34**(4), 399-416.

• China AI Development Report. (2023). *China's National AI Strategy: 2023 Update*. Tsinghua University.

• Feigenbaum, E. (2023). *AI and the New Cold War: The US-China AI Competition*. Carnegie Endowment for International Peace.

6. AI Ethics, Governance, and Regulation

• Bostrom, N. (2014). *Superintelligence: Paths, Dangers, Strategies.* Oxford University Press.

• O'Neil, C. (2016). *Weapons of Math Destruction: How Big Data Increases Inequality and Threatens Democracy*. Crown Publishing.

• Zuboff, S. (2019). *The Age of Surveillance Capitalism: The Fight for a Human Future at the New Frontier of Power.* PublicAffairs.

• UNESCO. (2021). *Recommendation on the Ethics of Artificial Intelligence.*

• European Commission. (2023). *EU AI Act: Comprehensive Regulation for Artificial Intelligence Development and Deployment.*

• Jobin, A., Ienca, M., & Vayena, E. (2019). *The Global Landscape of AI Ethics Guidelines.* Nature Machine Intelligence, **1**(9), 389-399.

7. AI's Impact on Financial Markets and Investment Strategies

• Brynjolfsson, E., & McAfee, A. (2017). *Machine, Platform, Crowd: Harnessing Our Digital Future.* W.W. Norton & Company.

• Nasdaq AI Trends Report. (2023). *AI's Role in Stock Market Predictions and Algorithmic Trading.*

• Financial Times. (2024). *The Impact of AI on Global Stock Markets and Investment Strategies.*

• World Economic Forum. (2023). *AI and the Future of Finance: Risk, Opportunities, and Ethical Considerations.*

www.ingramcontent.com/pod-product-compliance
Lightning Source LLC
Chambersburg PA
CBHW061356240926
51846CB00007B/1422
9786259734422